PROVERBS FOR
LEADERSHIP

You Must Understand Yourself & Improve
If You Desire Leadership
That Will Produce Success In Others

SEAN LITVAK

Proverbs for Leadership

Legal Disclaimer

Copyright © 2023 Sean Litvak. All rights reserved worldwide.

No part of this material may be used, reproduced, distributed, or transmitted in any form and by any means whatsoever, including without limitation photocopying, recording or other electronic or mechanical methods or by any information storage and retrieval system, without the prior written permission from the author, except for brief excerpts in a review.

This book is intended to provide general information only. Neither the author nor publisher provide any legal or other professional advice. If you need professional advice, you should seek advice from the appropriate licensed professional. This book does not provide complete information on the subject matter covered. This book is not intended to address specific requirements, either for an individual or an organization. This book is intended to be used only as a general guide, and not as a sole source of information on the subject matter.

While the author has undertaken diligent efforts to ensure accuracy, there is no guarantee of accuracy or of no errors, omissions, or typographical errors. Any slights of people or organizations are unintentional. The author and publisher shall have no liability or responsibility to any person or entity and hereby disclaim all liability, including without limitation, liability for consequential damages regarding any claim, loss, or damage that may be incurred, or alleged to have been incurred, directly or indirectly, arising out of the information provided in this book.

Scripture taken from the Modern English Version.
Copyright © 2014 by Military Bible Association.
Used by permission. All rights reserved.

Paperback ISBN: 979-8-9874291-0-5
Digital ISBN: 979-8-9874291-1-2

Praise for Proverbs For Leadership

Sean and Lauren Litvak are successful business leaders and influential Christian mentors. Lauren is an accomplished artist, and Sean is the Founder and Director of Litvak Leadership. They are some of the most positive individuals to be around. Over the years, they have trained themselves to speak words that release success, health, happiness, and prosperity. Sean shares from their own experiences and from God's Word, the Power of Your Words and that your input changes your output. This book is a must read that you will enjoy.
Dr. Bob Rodgers, Senior Pastor, Evangel World Prayer Center

The stories in our head become the stories of our lives. The words and messaging we choose to use will either propel us or hinder us. Sean Litvak, powerfully reminds all of us in 'Proverbs for Leadership' that we have the power to lift ourselves up. The road to prosperous living starts with our internal self-talk. Allow this book to be your tour guide to fulfillment and prosperity.
Larry Levine, author of Selling from the Heart, How Your Authentic Self Sells You

"In writing Proverbs for Leadership, Sean has developed an instructive, clear guide to approaching issues in life and work, through a lens of faith. Integrated with Scriptures and stories from his own journey, I believe you will find the book to be one that challenges you to courageously face things that can hold you back. Whether your desire is to grow in your career or personal life, Proverbs for Leadership is a resource I would recommend".
Dr. Jeff Williamson, CEO & Founder, Converge

Let me begin by saying that I am not a religious man. However, wisdom is where you find it. Only a fool would deny the value of studying the holy text.

Sean Litvak has plumbed the depths of the New & Old Testaments to find greater meaning in life and love. His selection of key quotes with personal commentary is on point for those determined to improve themselves and their lives through the accumulation of self-knowledge. His efforts will no doubt touch the lives of many in a very positive way.
Robert Bruce Adolph, Lieutenant Colonel, US Army Special Forces (retired) – author of "Surviving the United Nations," international speaker, and popular commentator

Sean has in this work, unearthed precious wisdom, not by random chance but by hard work, deep reflection and radical accountability. There is something here for everyone.
John H. Barrett, Executive Director, ISSA

I have known Sean for many years and have seen his hard work and determination in action. Sean has not been infallible, and he has learned through life experience to be a servant leader. What Sean has in spades is passion, and that shines through in his book and in his interactions with others. I believe that much can be learned from Sean's journey.
Nathaniel Shaw, private equity backed CEO and senior executive.

Proverbs for Leadership is a book for real people living in a real world. Do you desire to be a leader? Sean has provided a wealth of practical steps for us to apply in our lives to move us forward toward that goal. This is not "pie in the sky" platitudes. This is down to earth practical wisdom from someone who has lived it. Drawing from the Proverbs of Scripture, Sean provides a clear, contemporary presentation of that truth and how to apply it. I encourage you to take your time reading this book and begin applying what you learn right away.
Kevin McKnight, Executive Pastor, Evangel World Prayer Center, Louisville, Kentucky

Too often in our professional lives we are cautioned about showing emotion or leading from the heart. This book not only rebukes that idea but gives you the how-to guide needed to embrace your emotions and step in to the life you

are called with grace and professionalism. Sean Litvak has developed a contemporary lens through which you can explore your leadership style, challenge long held beliefs about spirituality in the workplace and discern your gifts. The ancient text of the Proverbs is a beautiful path for exploring your own leadership journey and Mr. Litvak's words will guide you in a way that you will feel supported.
Ronna-Renee Jackson, CEO/COACH/TRAINER, Launchpoint Leadership

I've known Sean within three associations. First as a fellow mastermind member. Second as a friend. And third as an author. I hope the associations continue to grow from there! Sean loves leadership and the scripture - and he's masterfully married them both in this book, Proverbs for Leadership!
Wes Wyatt, Founder of iEureka! and Host of the 'Market YOU First!' Podcast

When life throws you lemons, it's best to make lemonade. I was fortunate to have met Sean Litvak, an amazing man who has had, on several occasions, turned the lemons that showed up to challenge him and his faith into lemonade. He took on those challenges that came his way during the lockdown by turning his business activities to be a leader, inspiring others to thrive in the uncertainties of the pandemic. He did this virtually and in person. He faced a serious life-threatening health challenge and survived that. When he sets a goal, one that drives him, he is relentless. Learn from Sean's powerful faith-based experience that he shares in this book. You will learn from him what his get-to-iteveness and his stick- to-iteveness to continue on.
Phil Gilkes, Brian Tracy International Certified, Business Performance Coach /Sales Trainer and Facilitator

If you feel that you want to get to a better place personally or professionally, then you must read this wonderful book. It's filled with simple nuggets of truth and wisdom that will make you realize that you truly are the creator of your Success and Happiness.
Steve Rizzo- Bestselling Author of "Conversations with Bob"

I'm proud to call Sean Litvak a great friend! We originally met virtually via a mastermind group and later in person. I follow Sean not just as a friend but as an inspiration for loving a good life. Sean is a true leader who leads daily by example, not simply words. I truly enjoy his ability to take scripture in social media and this book, Proverbs for Leadership, and bring it to a meaningful "how to" live a full and blessed life.

Randy L Chaffee, CEO Source One Marketing, LLC, Host of Building Wins Live podcast

I want to endorse Sean Litvak's book "Proverbs for Leadership." There is so much valuable information Sean presents that's important for effective leadership. He shares his personal growth through the struggles we all face. "Do not correct a scoffer, lest he hate you; Rebuke a wise man, and he will love you. Give instruction to a wise man, and he will be still wiser; Teach a just man, and he will increase in learning." (Proverbs 9:8&9) Sean encourages prospective leaders to apply God's principles in everyday life. We need to confront our issues, if we're going to excel in our vocation. This is a compelling book that will challenge us to step up and be the best man and woman of God we can be. I like the stories connected to scripture, and the bullet point presentation. The chapter reviews help to reinforce the powerful truths he introduces. This is a must read for leaders and entrepreneurs in any field. Sean Litvak is a man of character and wisdom, and my friend and colleague. I'm getting several copies for me and my friends.

Mike Manuel, Evangelist and Christian Apologist, President of Revelation Power Ministries, faculty member of West Virginia Christian University

Proverbs for Leadership manages the increasingly rare feat of blending the practical and the spiritual into a seamless guide to becoming a better leader. With his dual focus on learning to lead yourself as well as others, Sean Litvak has written a smart and concise field manual for leaders looking for a path to greater success and influence.

Allen Howie, author, speaker, founder of Idealogy

The unique approach in this book is the constant encouragement to focus on others as the key to achieving our own goals. Particularly in this age of self-

focus it is refreshing to receive permission to give and receive encouragement, as well as to celebrate our God-given need for relationships, for accountability, and for positive influence. I particularly appreciate that Proverbs for Leadership is intentionally written from a Biblical lens, interwoven with personal lessons learned that makes each proverb completely relatable. Sean's willingness to share his own lessons with authenticity and transparency demonstrates a leadership courage many tout, but few truly possess.
Beth Gifford, President, The Human Resources Development Group

Proverbs of Leadership is chock full of pieces of advice, where the author shares the real-life lessons he has learned in his lifetime. You can read about the importance of your circle of influences and friends and how to control your anger. Sean shares the importance of faith in your life and how to strengthen your faith and avoid harmful triggers. This book can serve as your handbook to lead yourself and lead others.
Rich Filar, Business Communications Specialist at Quadient

"Proverbs for Leadership is a collection of timely, personal stories and Bible passages reminding us that being a good leader, indeed, being a good person isn't about going to church; it's about the value we create when we invest in ourselves and those around us, and follow our principles. Sean shows us how to make a lasting difference."
Dennis Mossburg, author of Reflections on Leadership, What Leaders say About Leadership and Director of Grey Moose Leadership Group, LLC.

I have struggled with focusing on relationships my entire life. Your book has made me realize I need to make time to foster relationships beyond my day to day business relationships. Proverbs of Leadership will help me reframe how I view my relationships with Faith, Family and Friends!
Dan W. Cline II, Executive Vice President, 4M Building Solutions, Inc.

In a world where so many are trying to tear us down, Proverbs for Leadership is a breath of fresh air. Sean recognizes that effective leaders have not only a strong business acumen, but also a solid foundation of faith, and

beautifully addresses how to cohesively meld them to enhance our lives, and the lives of those we mentor. This book is a must-read for any student of faith-based leadership.
Michelle Jessee Vincent, Vice President of Staffing, Ahead Human Resources

"Proverbs For Leadership" is a wonderful compendium for your faith library. It is full of Godly, practical wisdom that you can apply to your daily life starting today. Sean has spent a lifetime faithfully walking with Christ and seeking out His wisdom and has put the knowledge the Lord has given him in this book. Your faith and walk in the Lord Jesus will grow as you apply these biblical principles and you will be blessed.
Pastor Chuck Rodgers, Associate Pastor, Evangel North Church

God has entrusted a unique and powerful gift to Sean Litvak to speak the power of positivity to a world that has lost its way.
Leigh Ann Martin, Chaplain of Clark County Jail in Southern Indiana.

Simul Eximus—We go further together. This is the tone of Sean's work. To do so, we self-talk, exercise self-discipline, and hold ourselves accountable. There is much we do not control, but we all choose how we going to react to the stimuli in our life. This is about choosing wisely.
Colonel (Ret.) Joseph Frankie III, Author/President and Founder, JFIII Associates LLC

"This is a simple and real 'how to' walk day to day in life, based on teachings most all know and trust but haven't quite found a way to implement. Sean has succeeded in putting it together in a very easy, readable and concise manner. Now one only needs to counter those naturally occurring negative thoughts by spending a few moments with this. Well done!"
Brandon Lucas, Entrepreneur and Sales Executive

Sean Litvak has written a must-read guide to self-analysis and self-improvement through the paradigm of biblical wisdom. In this age of relativism and divisiveness, it is refreshing and encouraging to walk through Sean's applications of biblical truths to today's problems. Proverbs for

Leadership is a must read for you and a great gift for your young adults entering the business world.
Tony Young, P.E.

Proverbs are, by nature, short, easy to remember, and quotable. Sean delivers highly impactful life and leadership proverbs in a format you can consume in bites or in succession. Either way, you'll find yourself smiling as you relate to Sean's writing and connecting the dots within your own life.
Brad Bilen, Head of US 3P Direct Sales, Amazon Business & host of the "ManagerMirror" podcast

Proverbs for Leadership does an amazing job taking bible verses, which often can be difficult compare to our real life, and make them applicable to real scenarios. I found myself relating to Sean's stories and finding great biblical guidance. I wish I had the opportunity to read this earlier in my life.
Justin Clark, Vice President of Business Development, EVI Industries; Founder, Justinleadership

Sean Litvak has written a daily instructional process based on The Holy Scriptures. Proverbs for Leadership is truly a no-nonsense approach when you reference the word leadership. There is a summary section at the end of each chapter. All you need to do is simply make an effort to implement this daily process. The beauty of Sean's manuscript is that he offers a continual learning platform and not a one-time read. Sean is inviting you the individual reader to join this journey. Wisdom, let us be Attentive!
Mark W, Gassert, Sales Concepts, Senior Account Manager, ASEA Associate

I first met Sean Litvak as part of our business development mastermind group called MegaMind. Sean has always had a great passion for lifelong learning and community service. His support of family, friends and colleagues is a true testament to his belief in fellowship, stewardship and leadership, and the benefits of such.

In his book "Proverbs for Leadership" Sean continues to share the foundational, spiritual and motivational keys to creating a life of purpose and fulfillment, for being successful in achieving your endeavours, and to becoming a selfless, giving and supportive mentor and leader to those whom you share your life with. The book provides insightful and meaningful advice about the benefits of creating a healthy, holistic, faith based life so that you can be your "best self" and encourage others to succeed in their life's ambitions.

"Proverbs for Leadership" is a terrific resource, a book that I wholeheartedly encourage you to read, and refer to time and time again. Sean is sure to educate and inspire you, so that you can give your all to your family, your community, your organization and your team. That is leading by example.
Kim Hubbs, Megamind Member, Colleague; National Account Manager, Multigraphics

"Read it!" "Think it!" "Then live it!" "Proverbs for Leadership" contains some of the most applicable nuggets of truth I have ever read. Sean's writing brings a personal, insightful, practical level of personal "wisdom-thinking" into a perspective everyone can relate to. More importantly Sean's "wisdom writings" allows one to see very clearly how to rethink and embrace the truths related to the book of Proverbs, thus a new definition of leadership that can be applied to everyday situations we encounter in our personal and professional lives. You are now a "Proverbs Leader"
Thomas Ginn – President, Educo Group, LLC

Just as Proverbs is a book of wisdom, Sean's insight into the power of words in your life is a must read. He expertly explores which words you should allow into your life and which to ignore. Proverbs for Leadership is a quick read and a must for your personal library.
Pastor Bryan Veech, Louisville KY

This book is a must read for anyone interested in practical leadership from a biblical perspective. Sean presents useful tools to apply to everyday situations wrapped in wise precepts from foundational leaders.
Danny Short, Owner, Anchor Realty Services

Proverbs for Leadership is a must-have book! If you are looking for a book on leadership, look no further! This book contains the fruit you need to be rejuvenated and energized and will build your life skills at home, work, and in your walk with the Lord. It's a grand slam home run!

Titus 3:14, "Our people must learn to devote themselves to doing what is good, in order that they may provide for daily necessities and not live unproductive lives."
Kenneth W Mayberry, Servant of the Lord, Co-owner Annie's Pizza, Louisville, Kentucky

In Proverbs for Leadership, Sean gives you real-world examples and motivation to become a better person in and out of business. Being a man of faith myself, I can tell that the words were led by a higher power. This is a must-read book from a must-follow man of faith.
Tim Lord, Creative Director, Boston Impressions

Proverbs for Leadership

Sean Litvak

Table of Contents

Legal Disclaimer ii
Praise for Proverbs For Leadership iii
Table of Contents xiii
Dedication 1
Acknowledgments 3
Foreword 7
Introduction 9
Chapter 1: The Secret to Living a Life of Self-Talk 15
    Words Have Power 15
    Stronger Together 16
    The Value Of Friendship 18
    Internal Motivation 21
    Future Vision 21
    Summary of Chapter 1 24
Chapter 2: How to Overcome Triggers That Set You Off 25
    Anger Issues 25
    Change Your Input To Change Your Output 28
    Under Pressure 31
    Your Spiritual Anchor Is Your Foundation 32
    Summary of Chapter 2 33
Chapter 3: Strategies to Not Self-Sabotage 35
    Multiplying Your Way to Irritability: Physical Triggers 36
    Mental and Emotional Triggers 38
    The Benefits of Seeking Peace 40
    Summary of Chapter 3 43
Chapter 4: How to Stop Alienating People 45
    Leading A Team 45

- The ABCs: Attitude Beyond Collaboration 46
- Turning Dreams Into Reality 47
- Care For Your Community 48
- The Secret to Personal Peace, Understanding, And Contentment 50
- Summary of Chapter 4 52

Chapter 5: Mastering the Power of Listening and Moderation 53
- Bringing Your Best Self 53
- Meant To Be 55
- Summary of Chapter 5 61

Chapter 6: Living the Life of Discretion, Transparency, and Moderation 63
- Great Leaders Are Mature 63
- Summary of Chapter 6 69

Chapter 7: How to Make Moderation the Choice You Must Choose 71
- Thoughtful Communication 73
- Peace, Progress, Growth, or Regression? 74
- Your Approach Makes The Difference 75
- Summary of Chapter 7 78

Chapter 8: Avoiding Distractions Created by Feedback 79
- The Power Of Feedback 79
- "Thank You For Your Feedback." 80
- On A Mission, Or Wandering? 81
- Power Over Your Emotions 83
- Develop Roots And Build Strength. 84
- Summary of Chapter 8 86

Chapter 9: Scrutinizing Feedback and Motivation of Others 87
- Trust Develops Over Time - Do Not Allow Yourself To Become Jaded ... 87
- Be Aware Of The Idea Person Without A Plan 88
- Do Not Let Previous Experiences Block Possible Benefits 88
- Constructive Feedback Vs. Critical Feedback 90
- Be Warm, Tender, And Endearing 91

Speak To Others In An Honorable And Encouraging Way 91

You Reach Shared Goals When You Have Or Allow Many Ideas 92

Those Who Hold Themselves Unaccountable Are Driven By A Personal Agenda 93

The Inexperienced Sometimes Have The Clearest View 95

Summary of Chapter 9 96

Chapter 10: Why Thoughtful Consideration of Feedback is Important 97

The Personal Changes You Implement Will Create Different Outcomes 97

It's Normal To React Positively And Negatively To Feedback 98

Those Who Judge You Are a Gift 98

Feedback Is More Than What It Causes You To Think About 99

The Gratitude You Express to Others For Their Feedback Sets You Apart 100

Feedback Is Far More Than The Words Spoken 101

Viewing Feedback As Punishment Cuts You Off From Wisdom, Understanding, And Knowledge 102

Summary of Chapter 10 103

Chapter 11: Be Open to People Speaking into Your Life 105

You May Come Off As Arrogant Even When You Are Not 105

When You Are Not Self-Focused, You Will Listen To Almost Anyone 106

Your Willingness To Listen To Feedback Is What Sets You Apart From Most 107

The Way You Interact With Confrontation Is All About Personal Growth 108

Summary of Chapter 11 110

Chapter 12: Energy and Expectation Fuel Achievement 111

Even Being Friendly And Full Of Energy Has Its Challenges 111

Excuses Are The Drink Of Many In Society 112

Focus On Helping Others To Remove Mental Roadblocks 114

You Can Run And Hide, But Your Calling Remains 115

Embracing Your Calling Eventually Becomes Non-Work 117

Summary of Chapter 12 118

Chapter 13: Awareness is Balancing Self-Confidence and Admission of Your Flaws 119

Do Not Ignore Your Own Shortcomings. 119

Walking In Your Path Transforms You To Realize Your Potential 121

Listen To The Voice of God 122

Be All In 123

You Can Do Nothing Based On Strength Alone 124

Summary of Chapter 13 126

Chapter 14: Your Expectations Are Just for Yourself 127

Your Expectations Are Yours Alone 127

The Best Personal Expectation Is Moderation 129

Forgive The Other Person Of Their Offense 132

Summary of Chapter 14 133

Chapter 15: New is Not Always Better 135

New Is Not Necessarily Better 135

Everything Is Not Always Going To Go Your Way 136

Meet Obstacles With Joy 136

Make The Hard Choices 137

Be Sincere And Easily Understood 138

Revisit Your Calling 139

Summary of Chapter 15 141

Chapter 16: You Only Know What You Know 143

You Can Only Know What You Know 143

You Cannot Always Rely On Past Experience 144

Where Should You Look For New Ideas 144

You Need A New Attitude 145

Your Words Will Influence Others 146

Your Prejudices Are An Obstacle 147

Listen And Let Others Speak 148

Summary of Chapter 16 149

Chapter 17: Become a Productive Teammate 151

How To Become A Productive Teammate 151

Learn Lessons From Everyone 153

    Work With Excellence 154

    Do Not Focus On Fiefdoms 157

    Summary of Chapter 17 159

Chapter 18: Balance Response and Implementation 161

    How To Balance Feedback With Implementation 161

    Balance Introversion With Extroversion 163

    Do Not Be Enamored With The Sound Of Your Voice 163

    Summary of Chapter 18 167

Chapter 19: Self-Confidence is a Double-Edged Sword 169

    Self-confidence Can Be A Double-edged Sword 169

    Disagreement Does Not Mean Strife 171

    Determine True Value In Your Business Relationships 172

    Do Not Be Like The World 173

    Summary of Chapter 19 176

Chapter 20: Encourage Others to Speak 177

    Inspire Discussion During Meetings 177

    Create An Atmosphere For Voicing Opinions 178

    Facilitate The Sharing Of Ideas 178

    Develop Connections Between Teammates 179

    Anticipate Conflict Between Coworkers 180

    Be Patient With Everyone 180

    Do Not Shame Others 181

    Feedback Is A Structured Conversation 181

    Embrace The Conversational Process 182

    Summary of Chapter 20 183

Chapter 21: Listen More 185

    Make A Point To Listen Harder 185

    Misunderstandings Can Be Avoided 186

    Allow Others To Shine 187

    Plant The Seeds Of Listening 187

Do Not Isolate Yourself 188

　　Train Your Team To Exceed Your Abilities 188

　　Nurture Your Teammates' Gifts 189

　　Do Not Fear Feedback 190

　　Three Lessons 190

　　Summary of Chapter 21 192

Chapter 22: Create a Safe Place 193

　　Create A Safe Place For Ideas 193

　　Why People Fear Speaking Out 194

　　Do Not Take The Easy Path 196

　　Fear Is A Trap 197

　　Be Transformational 197

　　Build On Previous Ideas To Create Something New 198

　　Summary of Chapter 22 199

Chapter 23: Stares and Silence are Not Acceptable 201

　　Silence Is Not Acceptable 201

　　Ask Yourself Where You Failed 202

　　Build A Relationship With Those You Lead 202

　　Prepare More, Lead Less 203

　　Commit To Being Different 203

　　Be Honest With Yourself 204

　　The Measure Of Progress 204

　　Be Steadfast 205

　　Be Flexible 205

　　Learning Is A Process 206

　　Summary of Chapter 23 207

Chapter 24: Leading in a Vacuum Never Produces Results 209

　　Do Not Lead In A Vacuum 209

　　Complement Each Other 209

　　Growth Leads To Wisdom 210

Have Faith In Yourself	211
Coach For Excellence	211
How To Coach	212
Everyone Benefits	213
Summary of Chapter 24	214
Chapter 25: Do Not Become Frustrated	**215**
Avoid Frustration	215
Prepare For Criticism	216
Learn How To Critique Others	217
Practice Self-Control	218
Substitute Physical Exercise For Battle	219
Your Greatest Challenge	219
Build A Culture Of Collaboration	220
Summary of Chapter 25	222
Chapter 26: Shared Growth	**223**
What Shared Growth Means	223
Silence Is Not Golden	224
Find The Nuggets Of Truth	226
Ideas And Prosperity	227
Competence	227
Humility	228
Summary of Chapter 26	229
Chapter 27: How to Help Others Find Their Joy	**231**
Some People Are Never Happy	231
Working With An Unhappy Boss	232
Prepare For The Inevitable	232
Learn From Negative People	233
Understanding Pessimistic People	234
Encourage Accomplishing Of Goals	235
Prepare With A Positive Outlook	236

- Be Ready For Radical Changes 236
- Coach People Up Or Out 237
- Summary of Chapter 27 238

Chapter 28: Walking in Authority and the Responsibility that Comes with It. ... 239
- Beware Of Corporate Traps 239
- Coach To An Individual's Strength 240
- Learn From Your Trainees 241
- Remember Your End Goal 242
- The Right Time To Lead 243
- Summary of Chapter 28 245

Chapter 29: You will Always Need Additional Coaching 247
- Dealing With The Unexpected 247
- When The Coach Becomes The Student 248
- Passing The Mantle 249
- Thoughts On Self-Sabotage 251
- Generosity Of Spirit 251
- Summary of Chapter 29 253

Chapter 30: Set a Plan 255
- Know Your Teammates' Dreams 255
- Work On Assisting Others 256
- Recognize Your Flaws 256
- See The Potential In Others 257
- Leave The Past Behind 257
- The Challenge Of Selflessness 258
- Are You Ready? 259
- Summary of Chapter 30 260

About the Author: Sean Litvak 261

Dedication

I dedicate *Proverbs For Leadership* to my loving, caring, encouraging, and beautiful wife, Lauren. You have been my biggest cheerleader, standing by me through exciting times and disappointments even when you did not fully understand what I was doing. With your encouragement to always turn to God and His Word regardless of the circumstances or situation,

I know *Proverbs for Leadership* is written genuinely as "Sean inspired by God." You urged me to finish *Proverbs for Leadership* and challenged me to think through the following steps. I know God has great things for us to do together. Thank you for loving me and doing life with me!

Proverbs for Leadership

Acknowledgments

"If you write your book, I will have everything taken care of five times over." Those were the words that I heard God speak to me as I was frustrated and challenged with writing this book that He told me to write. It has taken much longer to write than I anticipated, but the lessons learned about myself, relationships, how to interact with others, and what it means to be a leader have been worth the wait. If you do not hear from God, I challenge you to get into a quiet place and listen. I wrote *Proverbs For Leadership* because I listened to God.

Who would have known all the challenges and growth I experienced over my career would become the stories I could tell, interspersed with biblical truth, and become a book? I am thankful for the companies I worked for during my career and those who have been my supervisors, managers, and leaders. Thank you for the opportunity to participate in leadership in a progressively increasingly meaningful way and for what working for you taught me about myself and how to lead people.

I also want to thank all the customers I have enjoyed working with over the years. Thank you for trusting me, allowing my employers and me into your facilities, and for what I learned about working through inevitable business challenges while serving you.

To my coworkers over the years, we may not have understood each other all the time, but looking back, I know your hearts were in the right place for the situations we faced together. We all wanted to be the best at what we were doing. We just approached it in different ways.

I am incredibly thankful for the Pastors and preachers I have met over the years that not only worked for God but also had their own businesses and taught me through example that life is not faith or business but can be both.

Thank you to my junior year high school honors English teacher, Dom Belmonte, who told me that whatever field I choose as a career better not include writing. That one statement alone inspired me to improve my writing skills. With what began in college and continued in business, never did I imagine at that time would turn into writing and publishing a book.

Thank you to Kim Thompson-Pinder and her teams at RTI Publishing. There is a saying, "the best is saved for last." After speaking with many publishers, I began to think that publishing did not have a heart and was only concerned about making money. You proved otherwise. Your willingness to work with me and encourage me to be true to myself created additional edits, delaying *Proverbs For Leadership*'s publishing but ultimately producing a book that reflects who I am.

To Megamind!, the mastermind group born during COVID, thank you for your support during one of my career's most challenging (exciting) times. When I told you as a group on ZOOM that I had felt like the odd misunderstood person amongst many of my coworkers for years, you responded that you understood me, and the problem was with those who did not understand me and not with me. Yes, I needed to be self-aware and not live in a vacuum, but I should not let haters get me down. You have all been an example of overcoming adversity and leaning into creativity.

To my children, Joshua, Elisabeth, and Meredith, who would ask periodically about "your book" and always have an encouraging word, even when I was not making the progress I desired. Thank you for believing in my writing.

Finally, to my wife Lauren, you have listened to me talk about everything in this book more times than I can remember, and you did it with amazement at how much I can talk. Without your support, encouragement, and patience, I would not have completed *Proverbs for Leadership*.

Sean Litvak

Inside *Proverbs For Leadership*, I poured my love for leadership, and the foundations of it, understanding yourself and improving. *Proverbs for Leadership* is my manifesto of understanding yourself and improving if you desire leadership that will produce success in others. You deserve to be the best version of yourself, and your team deserves the leader you will become from becoming that best version.

I hope you enjoy *Proverbs For Leadership*

Proverbs for Leadership

Foreword

It is amazing how a small thing can turn into something great. Little did I know that an invitation to be on a podcast would be the beginning of a business relationship that would last, but that is what happened between Sean Litvak and me.

When Sean asked if I would write the foreword to this wonderful book, I was honored. I have seen the impact of Sean's leadership skills and I am excited that he has put his knowledge into print. As an Accredited Executive Coach, and a Business Lecturer at the EU Business in Switzerland with 15 years experience it is easy to recognize true knowledge when I see it and this book is full of it.

As I read the book there were several things that personally impacted me and I know that if you take them to heart, they will change your life too. Some of them included being thoughtful of the sources that you allow into your mind. What goes in will come out in your self talk.

Listening is one of the greatest gifts that you can give yourself. As you increase the time you spend listening to others including your family, friends and co-workers the more your expertise will increase. One of the most essential people to listen to is yourself. What is going on internally? What is God saying to you? When those are master then your whole life will change.

You can only change yourself; you can't expect others to achieve something just because you want them too. Leading means setting an example and then encouraging others to follow. Ultimately, you are only responsible for your own choices.

Finally, never stop learning and planning. The person who does not set a plan for the future is destined to fail.

If you are looking to increase your leadership skills both personally and professionally then this book is for you. Sean gives you a strong foundation to help you become the leader that you are meant to be. He also shows you how to adapt your leadership style to be able to handle any scenario or situation you may find yourself in.

I highly recommend this book. It is easy to read and digest and the lessons are provided in bite size portions allowing you to make many small changes over a period of time.

Evan Tzivanakis,
Executive Coach / L&D Specialist / University Visiting Lecturer

www.executivecoachasia.com

Introduction

I was recently asked about how this book came to be written. Like most answers to a difficult question, my response was longer than just a few words.

How The Book Came To Be

Frankly, God told me to write this book. Specifically, He said, "If you write your book, I will have everything taken care of five times over." When I heard God say that, I thought He was talking about financial gain. You would think that would be enough motivation and encouragement to get someone to write their book. However, for me, at least, it was not.

My oldest file related to writing this book is from 2011. Then, there are a series of files that I wrote in both 2015 and 2016. In 2017, I decided to actually create an outline and not just write off the cuff. The outlining process continued well into 2018. My outlining style was finding Bible verses related to the chapter topics, and then writing my thoughts in tandem with the chapter topic and the Bible verses. I spent the balance of 2018 and all of 2019 writing. Obviously, I did not write as often as I should have to complete the manuscript quickly.

When 2020 came around, I was almost done writing the first draft, and then COVID-19 hit. You would think that I had the perfect timing to finish the first draft, but as I was already very comfortable with procrastinating on this writing project, I did not double down.

I found myself midway through the year in a mastermind group of individuals who challenged each other not to let COVID-19 hurt their business or personal goals, again forcing the writing of this book to the forefront. I finished my first draft in the third quarter of 2020 and then began the self-editing process, which became another way to procrastinate before publication.

As this was going on, I kept reminding myself of what God had said: "If you write your book, I will have everything taken care of five times over." I even tried to convince myself, unsuccessfully, that I was supposed to write the book but not necessarily publish it. I remember thinking that perhaps God wanted me to write this book to sort out my experiences, learn from them, not make the same errors again, and help others to avoid the mistakes I had made.

One day in July 2021, I spoke with my friend Clancy Clark, author of *Selling by Serving*, about the process I had gone through (and continued to go through), telling him I just wanted the book to be ready for any editor I chose. He paused, smiled, and told me to get over my fear, find an editor, and publish my book. His comment reminded me of what John Maxwell allegedly said about simply getting your first book completed: "Just finish it and know that it will take until you write your fifth book until someone thinks the first book you wrote is any good."

That led me to where I am today: writing this introduction to what has been a labor of love, dedication, discipline, frustration, elation, excitement, and, ultimately, personal achievement!

Here is one last story that will bring together all you have read in this introduction. I did move forward and hire a publisher to edit, proof, and guide me through the publishing process as Clancy Clark encouraged, and I was making significant headway. Then, in February 2022, I had an unexpected quintuple open heart bypass surgery. As I revisit this introduction in September 2022, I am very recovered; and I say "very" because too often, over the last six months, I have said I was fully recovered only to realize 30-60 days later how much more I have improved.

Recovery further delayed the completion and publishing of *Proverbs for Leadership*. Still, it did allow me to discover what God meant when He said, "If you write your book, I will have everything taken care of five times over."

I firmly believe that God was speaking about financial rewards, and He meant fully comprehending my experiences and helping others to avoid my mistakes. Ultimately, writing this book has allowed me to understand my calling, mission, and vision, and it brought wholeness, balancing the spiritual and earthly parts of my life.

The Main Themes Of This Book

This book is a manifesto of my journey in leadership, broken into two sections: "Know Yourself and Set the Bar High" and "Leading Without Frustration." In simpler yet expanded terms, this book is about understanding and coming to grips with one's own faults and areas of personal growth that must be achieved to improve yourself, which will make you qualified to lead others. Then, we discuss what to expect when you do lead others and how to respond appropriately to your expectations and interactions with those you are leading. There are a few reasons that the book is organized this way.

First, if you do not understand yourself and improve, you will never become a leader. You will instead stop that leader at every turn from emerging. Therefore, how you handle yourself (and then recognize how you are doing so), building upon strengths and overcoming weaknesses, is paramount.

Second, if I ask who the most crucial person in your life is, you may be demure and say someone else, but ultimately, pride creates that answer. In almost all situations, the most important person is yourself. Yes, there are circumstances where you can argue that point.

Still, when it comes to self-improvement, the benefits received, including the help your family will experience when you improve, will show even more that you need to focus on personal growth.

Third, the satisfaction you will get from growing personally should spur you on to further growth. If that does not encourage you, the thoughts of leveraging your growth to make a difference in the lives of others will help the most altruistic amongst us to take personal action.

It is a truism that it is lonely at the top, so why not take your team with you? More specifically, I mean your professional and personal team. The lessons each individual learns are only fully manifested when they can pass them on to others by coaching, supporting, and leveraging their growth.

To the non-leader, this sounds easy. To those who have had any leadership role, however, we know that some challenges come into play when attempting to guide a group. This is true regardless of whether you are associated with a group personally (family, faith, friends) or professionally (career, entrepreneurial pursuits, or associations).

The ultimate growth for the team and the individual occurs when personal development transfers to change within the group. The challenge is having the team engage and desire to grow beyond themselves and their leaders. Achieving that level of success is a win for everyone involved.

These are the primary themes of *Proverbs for Leadership*.

What To Expect and How To Best Use This Book

The reader can expect a book that is direct and to the point with each topic covered. Some of my peer editors said the book is structured as bullet-point style tough love, and not everyone may like that. I considered what they had to say and included far more personal stories as illustrations of the topics covered in this final edition.

If you are looking for a study that examines areas where I believe we all need improvement, how those improvements will affect your ability to lead, and how to pass that knowledge on to your team, then this is the book for you.

Throughout, I will address:

> - Self-talk and self-sabotage
> - How the words of people affect you
> - How your words affect others
> - How to be human and let people get to know you

- ➢ Feedback and how to embrace it
- ➢ Expectations, large and small
- ➢ Listening to your team
- ➢ Creating an atmosphere that motivates group engagement
- ➢ Your joy and the joy of your team
- ➢ Understanding the authority that you have been given
- ➢ Setting a plan to move ahead

How The Book Is Organized

I would encourage you to read the book in the order that the chapters are presented. This is not a how-to book in the sense that you can jump from one topic to another. Instead, each chapter builds upon the previous lessons, resulting in a process like climbing a mountain. You may take a helicopter to start in the middle, but you will then miss the training at the foothills that prepares you for the challenges ahead.

Thank you for deciding to buy and read *Proverbs for Leadership*. I hope you will be as blessed reading the book as I was in writing it. Each chapter opened up a greater knowledge of self that allowed me to understand why I was the way I was and how those lessons and experiences shaped me.

However, more importantly, armed with that wisdom, I attained an understanding that equipped me with the knowledge needed to move ahead in life, overcome obstacles and disappointments, and achieve dreams that will be built upon further.

Ultimately, I understood more about what God meant when He told me, "If you write your book, I will have everything taken care of five times over."

I hope you have that same experience!

Proverbs for Leadership

Chapter 1:
The Secret to Living a Life of Self-Talk

*The fear of the Lord is the beginning of knowledge,
but fools despise wisdom and instruction.
Proverbs 1:1*

*Be Thoughtful of the Sources You Allow into Your Mind.
They All Affect Your Self-Talk*

Words Have Power

You must learn to live a life of nourishing self-talk, which requires you to stop lying to yourself and embrace who you are. Once you do that, you can become and achieve much more than you ever realized is possible.

Break the programming of the words spoken over you.

Once, I thought I was not good enough to achieve my dream. I can still recall the words spoken to me many times as a child: "That mouth of yours is going to get you in trouble." "You talk too much. No one wants to hear what you have to say." "You are being unrealistic. Why do you think you could ever do that?"

Those words had programmed me for years and are still echoes that I have to fight, sometimes daily. Thankfully, I have overcome them primarily due to what I have learned during years of pursuing success. The lesson you must know is this: *Do not believe the lies of an unrenewed life.*

Those negative thoughts you allow yourself to experience are full of lies. You know them. They keep whispering that you are not good enough to perform at work, get that good grade in a class, buy the house, lead your family, have a happy marriage, or fulfill your calling.

Let me tell you something that you already know: those thoughts are lies, and buying into them is the easiest and deadliest thing you can ever do.

Stronger Together

Working alone is the slowest path to victory. For years, I took the path of least resistance. It is easier to buy into the lies that your mind manufactures than it will ever be to push through them and do what needs completion. I eventually realized that to move forward, I needed to make changes and stop trying alone to be the best person that I knew, deep down, I could be.

We all need counselors and collaborators in our lives. To do what needs to be done, you need collaboration. It would help if you had counsel. It would be best if you had a circle of influence. Where are you receiving counsel? If you paused for long after the question, it means from no one.

Do yourself a favor, and find a few people you trust to act as your counselors.

> "And if someone might overpower another by himself, two together can withstand him. A threefold cord is not quickly broken."
> Ecclesiastes 4:12

Call them your circle of influence. Ask them to hold you accountable within a particular area where you desire to accomplish something. The positive feedback, encouragement, and constructive criticism they provide will motivate you to stop lying to yourself.

My historical circle of influence comes from different years of my life. I am blessed that I have a circle of influence in my life. My circle of influence is seven men that come from various geographies and backgrounds. I have not seen some of them in person for years and only speak on the phone occasionally.

This circle of influence includes two of my oldest friends, a business partner I was assigned to work with fifteen years ago, a friend from a church that my wife and I attended over twenty years ago, a small group leader from another church that my wife and I attended for a short while, a former work supervisor turned friend. A business owner I met at yet another church.

Some I would call close friends, but most are no longer close friends. Although I am not in regular contact with most of these men, I know that they will make time for me, and they know that I will make time for them. Writing this book made me realize who my circle of influence was. This is not the same circle of influence I had in high school, college, our early marriage years, or our marriage child-rearing years.

Recently I was welcomed into a new group of collaborators and counselors, and yes, they are a current circle of influence. As I review my writing during the COVID-19 pandemic, I realize that my circle of influence has changed. I am part of a mastermind group that has become a significant circle of influence in my life. There are twenty-three of us.

I am influenced by some more than others, but I am affected by all of them. They are a circle of influence I was not seeking and did not expect to find. Honestly, they are a group of people more like myself than I thought existed.

We all have the resource of a circle of influence to encourage us. Do not tell me that you do not know anyone who should be in your circle of influence. Everyone has at least one person, and usually multiple people, in their life: a teacher, mentor, friend, or co-worker, for example.

You need to take the bold step of bringing others into your life who will collaborate with you in the slightest way to hold you accountable so you can stop lying to yourself about your abilities and the actions needed to reach your goals.

Don't Be A Fool: Allow And Trust Collaborators To Influence Your Life.

If you try to do alone whatever it is that you desire, then you are a fool.

> *"Hear counsel and receive instruction,*
> *that you may be wise in your latter days."*
> *Proverbs 19:20*

I'm not suggesting you tell everyone what you want to achieve, just select individuals (your circle of influence) who will encourage and hold you accountable.

Whom do you respect? Who will give you the advice and instruction you are willing to accept and you know will produce results in your life if followed? Those are the few people you need to surround yourself with to become the person you desire to meet in the mirror each morning.

The encouragement you receive is based on whom you place yourself around.

The encouragement of your circle of influence will lead to positive self-talk replacing the lying-to-yourself talk you have done. The advice received from your circle of influence and the self-talk it produces in you will be healthy and fuel your mind, will, and emotions. Your improved, healthy, fully fueled mind, will, and emotions will create more significant moderation in your life.

The Value Of Friendship

> *" Iron sharpens iron,*
> *so a man sharpens the countenance of his friend.*
> *Proverbs 27:17*

Your choice of friends affects your life trajectory. You are the average of your five closest friends. If that is the case, your choices of friends and associates have far greater significance than you realize. I have always found that the best friendships are with those who challenge me, not with sarcasm or negativity, but in a way that invigorates me to become more than I realize I am capable of becoming.

Do not be surprised when friendships change over time. Friendships are hard. I believe they become more difficult the older you grow. When you are younger, the world is full of opportunity, and the person who has given up on life is far less common in your circle of friends. The closest group of friends I ever had was when I was in college and the two years immediately after graduation. We had each other's backs and supported one another. As life moved forward for each of us (we got married one by one) and my wife and I moved to another city 350 miles south, we lost the familiarity with one another.

As you move through life, it is all the more vital that you pay back the encouragement you received from others. When you have received the support you desired, it is even more reason to pay it forward and become an encourager of others. Plant those seeds of encouragement in others and reap the rewards of becoming much more than you realize.

Your encouragement of others will draw people around you. Encourage others, and you will not only never be at a loss for friends, but you will find people of the same thought processes becoming attracted to you. Make them your squad, posse, close friends, or members of your circle of influence. Surrounding yourself with encouragement only happens when you are an encourager.

Your vision will be expanded or diminished by whom you choose as friends.

Back in college, I joined a fraternity. There were both positive and negative experiences, but what I learned during those days was how small my vision was. I was surrounded by new friends from much wealthier means than I did.

For most of them, having money and the thought of what to spend it on was never a question they even considered. My fraternity brothers made me realize how much more there was that I could accomplish. This was the catalyst of realizing my past thoughts about success and that my future needed to be revitalized.

Friends Tell The Truth

Friends will tell you exactly what they think of your ideas. Not only will you become more than you realized, but you will also receive encouragement, a sounding board, a gut check, or simply counsel. You need someone (and even better, a group) to hear what you have to say and tell you when your idea is stupid. Frankly, the grand ideas created in the vacuum of your mind are only sometimes as good as you think them to be.

Pitch out loud that last glorious idea you had to someone you have permitted to speak honestly about your life. Do not ask your spouse, as they have a vested interest in keeping the peace with you. See what your circle of influence members thinks of your great idea. How does it sound when said out loud? Are you able to defend your plan from the holes that your circle of influence may find in it?

Your friends are part of your circle of influence. Understand me clearly. Only you know what your calling is and what achievements you desire, but your circle of influence will force you to be honest with yourself. You can plant seeds, but what is going to grow from your efforts is best funneled by a trusted circle of influence who want to see you achieve, just as you want to see them succeed.

Align yourself with the like-minded, right-minded, and sound-minded circle of influence in your life, and the plans you put in place will be those that propel you to become far more than you realize.

Another benefit of allowing others into your life is that their influence creates moderation. This moderation keeps you from the emotional highs and lows. The emotional swings from the past have made you lie to yourself. Now, you will experience the satisfaction and joy that comes from walking in your calling through the encouraging collaboration of your circle of influence, not the driving force of supposed self-motivation.

Sean Litvak

Internal Motivation

"And whatever you do, do it heartily, as for the Lord and not for men, knowing that from the Lord you will receive the reward of the inheritance. For you serve the Lord Christ."
Colossians 3:23-24

Personal motivation will never be replaced by the influence of others. Please do not misunderstand me. You need personal motivation to complete your calling. Still, it will never happen without the collaboration of a circle of influence in your life; they will help you stop lying to yourself and move forward. Once you step forward, you will walk knowing who you are.

The path of least resistance leads to a muddy mess. The path of least resistance is embracing the lies of self-deception. Only a fool stays in that place, running down the rabbit hole deeper and deeper, only to get stuck. Embrace who you know you are, not who you once were. You have left the defeating self-lies of the past behind, so embrace the person you are today.

Future Vision

Leave the past behind and walk forward in expectation. Walk in the plans of your future without looking back. These are the plans to experience prosperity in ways you do not even comprehend today. The person you are now is enough to produce the success of your current calling.

Do not concern yourself with how you will handle what is ahead.

"Therefore, take no thought, saying, 'What shall we eat?'
or 'What shall we drink?' or 'What shall we wear?'
(For the Gentiles seek after all these things.) For your heavenly Father knows that you have need of all these things."
Matthew 6:31-32

Knowing who you are, feeling all there is, and embracing the success of today will prepare you for tomorrow. Walk in that expectation.

How do you speak about yourself and your plans for the future? Allow yourself to speak with bold expectations but expect naysayers. Speak with the confidence of you knowing who you are [as a child of God] and in the expectation of [one who serves a God who keeps His promises]. Do not allow yourself a lazy life of self-deprecation.

> *"Then Moses said to the Lord,*
> *"O my Lord, I am not eloquent, neither before nor since You have spoken to Your servant. But I am slow of speech, and of a slow tongue." The Lord said to him, "Who has made man's mouth? Or who made the dumb, or deaf, or the seeing, or the blind? Have not I, the Lord? Now therefore go, and I will be with your mouth and teach you what you must say." He said, "O my Lord, send, I pray, by the hand of whomever else You will send."*
> *Exodus 4:10-13*

Be bold, ready, and willing to proclaim for all to hear, along with yourself, who you are. This is something I had to overcome time and again due to being told over and over that my mouth would get me in trouble. The expectations that I spoke were too much for some to understand. Know that you will receive pushback from others when you decide to take the path less traveled that leads to success and not self-pity.

Focus On Today, Hope For Tomorrow

The best decision you can make now is to **focus on today**. It is not your understanding of tomorrow or even the moment that matters. It is your self-awareness, emotional awareness, knowledge, and wisdom that produce the results you desire tomorrow. Focus on today.

Tomorrow will be provided for by the seeds you plant today and the understanding of self you decide to walk in and through.

> *"But seek first the kingdom of God and His righteousness, and all these things shall be given to you. Therefore, take no thought about tomorrow, for tomorrow will take thought about the things of itself. Sufficient to the day is the trouble thereof."*
> *Matthew 6:33-34*

Today is a day to enjoy yourself in your calling. Enjoy the day; you were made for it. Have you ever met anyone enjoying themselves who has ultimately failed? I have met plenty of people walking in a depressed spirit that fail, but not those who walk in joy. Delight in who you are and the calling of your life. It is unique to you, and only you know what it is and how to execute it.

Walking in your calling produces victory. The moment you allow yourself to walk in whom you know you are, you will have patience in your life, for yourself, and your plans. The tasks that once seemed mundane will ultimately produce your desire and will become exciting stepping stones calling your name.

All victories must be celebrated and then built upon. Small victories that seemed insignificant will come into a more unobstructed view of how they build upon one another to reach your desired goals based on the calling born within you. Knowing who you are will free you from the prison of untapped and unembraced potential, propelling you instead to achieve your goals.

Your life will be challenging if you want it to produce rewards. What I describe is not a life for the weary and faint-hearted. Be bold, strong, and expectant. Are you ready to embrace whom you know you are and become much more than you realize?

Summary of Chapter 1

1. You and only you can break the programming of the words spoken over you. Your programming will change if you live a life that the Word of God renews. Do not believe the lies of an unrenewed life.
2. Make an active choice about the people you allow to speak into your life. Listen to the truths spoken to you from your circle of influence. You may not like what they say, but you have given them the right to be part of your inner circle to influence. Remove those people from your life who do not encourage or motivate.
3. Your motivation must be fueled by your vision for the future and not looking back at failures you have experienced. Failure will teach valuable lessons, but it does not motivate you to achieve your vision.
4. Like the steps you made yesterday determined today, the actions you take today will define tomorrow. So, focus on today and have expectations for tomorrow.

How long, you simple ones, will you love simplicity?
For the scorners delight in their scorning,
and fools hate knowledge.

Proverbs 1:22

Chapter 2:
How to Overcome Triggers That Set You Off

*My son, if you will receive my words,
and hide my commandments within you,
so that you incline your ear to wisdom,
and apply your heart to understanding.
Proverbs 2:1-2*

You have personal triggers that set you off in the wrong direction emotionally. Do not let the triggers whip you around like a dog wags its tail.

Anger Issues

Anger is a serious challenge that I have experienced over my life. "Experienced" probably does not describe the challenge appropriately. Better said, anger is something that I have struggled with during my lifetime. That is the bad news. The good news is that I have become a far more moderate, happy, and civil person as I have gotten older. However, I do not think it has anything to do with age.

We all know grumpy old men, and the word "curmudgeon" certainly does not portray someone as warm and fuzzy. I have learned over the years that to avoid anger, I need to either avoid or respond differently to those things that set me off.

Guard Yourself Against Anger

You know the drill. You are working toward completing a project, trying to achieve a goal. Sometimes, it happens when you are working with other people. Other times, it happens when you are working alone. Ultimately, it happens because you let it happen. You let your guard down and allow yourself to get set off. However, it is not like the thing that angered you did the work itself. No, becoming angry is something you have chosen to embrace. I know this from personal experience.

You Create Your Own Struggles

When I allow myself, I can be very particular about everything. I was one of those people that thought my way was always best. Because I was like that, I struggled when others did not approach solving a problem the same way I would or thought best. It did not matter if the person was a subordinate, counterpart, or supervisor. I struggled when the conclusion they came to for handling issues and challenges was not what I thought was correct.

Do not give in to the temptation of responding negatively. Let me stress: it is not the people you work with or the situation you find yourself in that sets you off. It is you giving in to temptation and allowing yourself to be set off. You will experience temptation. The cure is to know what sets you off so you can overcome it.

The Anger You Fight Is Common To Everyone; Learn To Control It

The rise of anger within yourself is not unique to you; it is familiar to everyone. What is uncommon is someone embracing their ability to walk in a moderated, even contemplative life while still working to achieve their dreams, goals, and plans because they have identified and overcome what sets them off.

> *"No temptation has taken you except what is common to man.*
> *God is faithful, and He will not permit you to be tempted above what you can endure but will, with the temptation, also make a way to escape, so that you may be able to bear it. So, my beloved, flee from idolatry.*

Sean Litvak

I speak as to wise men. Judge for yourselves what I say."
1 Corinthians 10:13-15

Distill Anger Into Personal Wisdom Of Self-Control And Passion

You can exhibit self-control without having it drain the life and excitement out of you. You have spent the better portion of your life learning, accepting correction, and absorbing knowledge. You now need to distill that knowledge into personal wisdom for self-control.

Self-control and restraint are not the same things. Self-control is not what you experience when sitting in front of the computer, phone, television, or reading a book. Self-control is defined as related to emotions, desires, and expressions of them, especially in difficult situations and events. Restraint is when you have the power to be fully engaged in an activity; moderate behavior, staying within limits daily. The action could be either work or non-work related. You have all experienced being set off inside and outside of work situations.

Self-control is what many on social media lack.

"He who has no rule over his own spirit
is like a city that is broken down and without walls."
Proverbs 25:28

Self-control is having the courage not to give in to the wound-up spring within you driving you to anger. It is easy to give in to the spring. Everyone does it, especially now. Look at social media. People revel in allowing themselves to be set off. The complete lack of in-person social interaction in social media is a driving force in what enables people to say what they do, respond to others how they do, and ultimately lose self-control. For this reason alone, if I find myself in a social media conversation where there is an obvious difference of opinion, I ask myself how my words would be understood out of context. If the answer is negative, I do not post the response but write it again and again until it is kind.

Change Your Input To Change Your Output

Do something instead that will put you outside the typical group of people that allow themselves to set off. Change what you read, watch, and listen to. Everything you expose yourself to influences how you will respond to others, including this book.

Walking in fear produces negative outcomes. When you walk in fear and anxiety of people, projects, outcomes, and judgments, you set yourself up to behave like a pressure cooker that will eventually explode. Do you want to release all that pressure in a healthy way? The good news is that you can do so.

Did you get angry during the pandemic? During the COVID-19 pandemic, I had great opportunities to give in to anger because things were beyond my control. How I responded to that anger is a testament to my faith journey through the last thirty years. Was I perfect? No. Was I far better than I would have been in the distant and recent past? Absolutely.

Stop critically judging others, and you will become a happier person. Stop being critical of others.

> *"Let no unwholesome word proceed out of your mouth, but only that which is good for building up, that it may give grace to the listeners."*
> *Ephesians 4:29*

It is that easy. If you stop judging others because of what you see as their inability to perform to your standards, you will become a much more moderate, consistent person that does not anger easily. The first step to not being set off is to give up the false control you have given people over your life. When I implemented this process in my daily walk, it was life-changing.

The lifestyle of continuous pursuit leads to frustration and anger. If your primary motivation in life is accumulating wealth and things, you will always be pursuing more rather than enjoying what you have already earned. Living that lifestyle opens you up to becoming controlled by the non-issues in your life.

Every Time You Pass A New Hurdle, You Realize There Is Another Challenge

Think about where you are today. There was a time in your life when you thought that if you could achieve more, all your needs would be taken care of, and you would not have any worries. If you are reading this book, you are the person who strives to improve. How is that working out for you? Are you at the point where your concerns are non-existent or have you discovered that when you have increased responsibility, there is more for you to do and more people who depend on you?

There will always be trials in your life, regardless of how successful you have become. Success is very relative. The level of success you have today would have brought you comfort three, five, or ten years ago, yet today you strive for even more. Have you taken the time to sit back and enjoy the fruits of your labor and sacrifices, or are you so focused on achieving more; that you are creating issues in your life where there are not any? Let the fruits of your labor make you steadfast, satisfied, and free from torment.

The Challenge Of Success Is Thinking You Always Need To Push For More

I once heard someone say that the more you earn, the more you spend. I immediately knew that to be true but did not see the further implications. The greater your success, the greater your desire for success and achievement will become, and the increasing pressure you will experience to repeat and expand that performance. The further I have moved along in my career, from simple projects to those of greater complexity and responsibility, the greater the pressure has been. The pressure I have experienced has not just been for myself to succeed but also for the teams I led. Each success brings the temptation to push harder.

> *"Now faith is the substance of things hoped for,*
> *the evidence of things not seen."*
> *Hebrews 11:1*

Faithlessness and fear reveal that you think you have not succeeded. You may believe that if you are not focused on continuously achieving, everything you have completed will slip away. That is faithlessness at the root of your success. Frankly, if you think that way, you have failed. Instead, be sober-minded and know that giving in to the theoretical issues you have imagined and the dissatisfaction you feel is not worth the effort. It is an easy way out. Instead, be strong, take the high road, and let your striving for success be a non-issue.

Share your struggles with people you trust. Stay focused and out of your head. If you do not know how to do that, then ask for help. Collaborate with your circle of influence. Share with them your struggle to be satisfied while striving for more and how you are making non-issues into conflicts. The conversation started will most likely echo truths back at you and surprise you at how common what you are experiencing is to your circle of influence.

Trusting and working with others is a braided rope. You can get a lot done on your own, but like a braided rope, you are much more reliable in collaboration with others. Be willing to open yourself up and be vulnerable to people you trust. Do not look at this as a weakness but rather a strength. The flaw is in thinking about and doing things the same way when the results do not change. Instead, celebrate the strength you have shown in the willingness to share with your circle of influence your struggles with imaginary problems and how you seek to overcome them.

"There is nothing new under the sun"
Ecclesiastes 1:9b.

Although you may not believe it, your situation is like everyone else's. It exists to you and creates a temptation to be distracted and eventually set off. Regardless of the situation, you are currently experiencing, do not let it have control over you. Instead, you can take control through moderation and realistic expectations of problems that set you off.

Sean Litvak

*"Let your eyes look directly forward,
and your gaze be straight before you."
Proverbs 24-25*

Under Pressure

When I feel pressure, I am glad I have built a foundation in my faith. Reading the accounts of biblical figures and how they were wrought with pressures and temptations has inspired me. Truly, they are examples reminding me that there are never any new challenges.

A life without a grounding in faith is worthless. Be moderate in your responses because you have positive expectations for the future. Your expectation needs to be grounded in something other than yourself or another person. Yes, I am talking about having and making a spiritual anchor a part of your life. For me, that is my faith as a Christian and a follower of Jesus Christ. For you, it may be something else. If all you do is rely on other people, you will continuously be disappointed, frustrated, set off, and eventually fail in every situation.

Do not be surprised when you experience fear. Whatever situation you are in, your faith should comfort you, make you secure, give you courage, and allow you to overcome fear regardless of the issue. Like most of us, you have the potential to experience anxiety and fear.

The most fearful people I know rely solely on others and not on their faith. The second most fearful people are those who claim to have faith but refuse to exercise it regularly during peaceful times. Then, in challenging situations, they are already walking in faithlessness; they are set off in fear. They say whatever pops into their head, and what usually goes straight from head to mouth is influenced by fear. It is said that fear is "false evidence appearing real." Do not make permanent decisions based on temporary situations.

*"For God gave us a spirit not of fear
but of power and love and self-control."
2 Timothy 1:7*

Do Not Make Life-Altering Decisions When You Are Fearful

So many people make life-altering decisions in fear over their situation instead of embracing their existence as a mortal, and living a life with a spiritual anchor. I am not telling you that those with a spiritual anchor are perfect. I have a perspective that eludes those who depend on people instead of their faith.

However, I was not always this way. I made a life-altering decision in my thirties that marked me for a lifetime. That decision to move forward in a specific direction was based solely on fear. Even with the counsel I received, no one could tell me I was wrong, just that they were not going to take the same decisive action I was planning to and eventually took. At that time, I missed my circle of influence who could tell me that I was wrong, but in a very nice way. I learned that I needed to read between the lines of any answers given.

Your Spiritual Anchor Is Your Foundation

You will have trouble, and challenges will come your way but know that with your spiritual anchor, you can weather the storm. Let your spiritual anchor be your strength. The strength you possess when in faith is far more substantial and real than any power you think you get from people. Use your faith to have the strength you need to avoid being set off. Instead, face every situation with moderation and positive expectation.

Follow this advice, and you will become the person you need to be to succeed in all areas of your life.

Summary of Chapter 2

1. You are creating struggles when you give in to anger. Be on guard against anger and the triggers that cause it for you.
2. Everyone has triggers that will set off personal anger. What separates people is the understanding of their triggers.
3. Your willingness to open up to someone in your circle of influence about what triggers you and where you struggle will create the collaboration needed that builds strength through vulnerability.
4. Renewing your mind with God's Word will help you overcome triggers and reveal the further challenge of triggers you did not know you needed to overcome.
5. God's Word that you allow to influence and change you will adjust your foundation and anchor you through the storms of life, especially those you bring on yourself.

*So, you may walk in the way of good men
and keep the paths of the righteous.*

Proverbs 2:20

Chapter 3:
Strategies to Not Self-Sabotage

Do not be wise in your own eyes;
fear the Lord and depart from evil.
It will be health to your body,
and strength to your bones.

Proverbs 3:7

The actions you take against yourself, even in the name of relaxing and recharging, are still actions against yourself.

We all must learn the difference between personal enjoyment and self-sabotage.

Explore What Will Eventually Set You Off

In the last chapter, I talked about the people and habits you allowed to affect you negatively. Now, I will explore things you do to yourself that eventually set you off. In other words, how do you self-sabotage?

There is more that derails you than you realize. Mental roadblocks can prohibit you from achieving your dreams and goals and considering others and their needs. However, there are also physical habits that can derail you from moving forward. Let us look at some of them.

No One Can Exercise For You

Sloth, slovenliness, laziness, and getting out of shape are physical habits that keep you from moving ahead. I have exercised on and off for more than 35 years. When I exercised regularly, I always had the best attitude about life, was the friendliest toward people, and had the most substantial confidence in myself. I may occasionally have overdone it and strained a muscle along the way. Still, that pain was nothing compared to the suffering of feeling and being fat, tired, unmotivated, and avoiding my reflection in the mirror.

> *"Slothfulness casts into a deep sleep, and an idle soul will suffer hunger. He who keeps the commandment keeps his own soul, but he who is careless in his ways will die."*
> Proverbs 19:15-16

When you feel overweight, tired, and lazy and avoid looking at yourself in the mirror, do you get anything worthwhile accomplished? A better question is: when you are not exercising, do you want to do anything useful that will challenge you and create momentum? How about when you are working out and commanding your body to your will instead of being subject to it? When you subject your body to your will, you win and accomplish much!

Multiplying Your Way to Irritability: Physical Triggers

Now that I have laid out how it feels to allow yourself to get out of shape due to laziness let's look at a multiplier that makes your idle self even more irritable.

Is The Time Invested In Alcohol Really Worth The Return?

Drinking too much alcohol or being plain and straightforward drunk will not get you where you want to go. Too much alcohol will also have a negative physical effect on you. Frankly, any alcohol will keep you from achieving anything of consequence for the remainder of the day. I am not advocating abstaining from drinking any adult beverage. To do that would be hypocritical.

I advocate for accomplishing everything you want to achieve for the day before having an adult beverage. I am also reminding you that too much of anything has a negative impact, which is especially true with alcohol. Other than the immediate loss of inhibitions and the ability to drive, the possible experience of a hangover the next day will have a further lasting derailment on your dreams, goals, and plans. Worse yet, when you have too much to drink, and your body rejects the alcohol before you know it, you are down on your hands and knees, puking in the toilet or lying on the bathroom floor because the cold hard tile feels good.

I am saddened to report that we have all been there. I remember what it was like to be happy that the cold hard tile floor gave me solace. Looking back, I see that I was totally and completely out of control and needed self-knowledge and emotional intelligence to understand the myriad of emotions I was experiencing. Instead, I drank too much and learned nothing. Alcohol is an escape and a reaction to a lack of personal understanding. Do not go there; instead, behave moderately. Your relationship with food can be like that with alcohol.

My Own Personal Hell Is Overeating

"For the drunkard and the glutton will come to poverty, and drowsiness will clothe a man with rags."
Proverbs 23:21

Yes, I have gone through periods without working out and have had too much to drink on occasion, but the most consistent physical trigger I have chosen (yes, I said chosen) to embrace is overeating. Overeating is worse than the previous two negative habits.

Letting yourself get out of shape is all about food and wondering what is next to eat. Unless you are in the direst of straits, you do not need to concern yourself about where your next meal is coming from. Real hunger can derail a person, but for some, it creates a lack of motivation to move ahead. Those who eat themselves to obesity will find they are too tired to accomplish anything worthwhile. I am not talking about medical conditions, but rather worshiping food like it is God and acting like eating is your sacrament.

Emotional Highs And Lows Distract You Physically

The responsive emotional highs and lows available to you in every situation have a physical impact on moving ahead. The extreme highs and lows are particularly distracting, physically intoxicating, and create inner pain, all at the same time. The moderate response to any situation does not mean behaving without passion. Feel the emotional high or low, but then move ahead in a controlled way to overcome the negative physical habits. Nothing lasts forever, so stop acting as though it does.

Those are the physical body triggers. Now, let us look at other types of mental and emotional triggers.

Mental and Emotional Triggers

Just as food and alcohol can lead to situations that trigger negative behavior, our habitual thoughts and careless speaking can lead to mental and emotional triggers that create unnecessary stress in our lives.

You Do Not Need To Have The Last Word

I needed to bring my mouth under moderation and realized that I could not just say whatever popped into my head. That is something I have had to learn, sometimes the hard way, and it is a lesson I remind myself of daily. Why? Because speaking every thought, you have will lead to arguments. Nothing will derail your dreams, goals, and plans more than strife. It is of all importance to maintain peace, as best you can, with everyone you interact and engage.

Give Peace With Everyone A Chance

Peace with everyone you engage is indeed a lofty expectation to put on yourself; however, what are the alternatives?

> *"There is one who speaks like the piercings of a sword, but the tongue of the wise is health."*
> *Proverbs 12:18*

You might ask, what about being at peace with one-third of the people we engage with? If that is too low, then how about being at peace with 85% of the people we interact with? If that seems to be a more reasonable number, then tell me, with which 15% are you not going to be at peace?

Peace And Harmony Are Always Better Than Bitterness And Strife

Choosing to be enemies with some people is far harder than doing whatever you can to be at peace with everyone. Not only is it a much better experience for those you come into contact with, but it is also a personal attitude that promotes a better life for yourself. When you are not in harmony with someone, you are sowing the roots of bitterness and strife within yourself. Ultimately, those roots will rot within you and create personal trouble. Sowing roots of pain and conflict will cause you to become even more judgmental towards a more significant number of people. It is best instead to plant roots of peace, not bitterness and strife.

Be Kind To Everyone, Period

If instead of bitterness and strife, you choose to be kind to everyone you come into contact with, imagine how your attitude will improve and what your reputation will become. At the time I am editing this book, we are almost three months into the COVID-19 pandemic of 2020. Never before in my life have I had to moderate myself so much when engaging with others. Truly, every interaction has the potential to be unexpected and delve into unknown conversations.

The tenderness that you display will have a positive effect on others. Your tender-heartedness will encourage people to enjoy being around you, creating life-long, positive interactions that launch, inspire, direct, and promote your dreams, goals, and plans.

Judge And You Will Be Judged

The alternative is to live a life of judgment of others on how they live, talk, interact, think, etc. Who are you comparing them to as the example of a better way to live? Yourself? The judgment you have for others will occur against you.

"Judge not, that you be not judged.
For with what judgment you judge, you will be judged,
And with the measure you use, it will be measured again for you"
Matthew 7:1-2

The Benefits of Seeking Peace

The Forgiveness You Show Others Will Come Back To You

Instead of judging others, live a life of forgiveness and seek to be at peace with everyone. When that becomes your reputation, others will think twice before judging and thinking ill of you. With a reputation of seeking peace with others, avoiding strife, and being kind, people will work to be the same way toward you.

The lack of distraction allows time for personal achievement. Without the distraction of giving into those attitudes and thoughts that derail progress, you will be able to work on your dreams, goals, and plans, ultimately living the life you desire, achieving what you want, and helping others.

Your Approach Is The Key To Success

Avoid at all costs the physical habits and attitudes that will sabotage your dreams, goals, and plans. Your approach is up to you. You must keep your position positive or, as some say, on the high ground. How is this done? By avoiding anything evil.

Be In The World, But Not Of The World

"I am to be no longer in the world, though these are in the world, for I am coming to You. Holy Father, through Your name keep those whom You have given Me, that they may be one as We are one."
John 17:11

I am not telling you to live life in a cabin in the woods away from all influences that have the potential to corrupt. Sequestering yourself apart from all forces considered evil would result in you becoming self-focused, thus depriving others of the benefits they would receive knowing and interacting with you. As a result, you will be denied a life of growth through experience.

Instead of self-sabotage, promote your dreams, goals, and plans. Rather than self-sabotage, live the life where you ask yourself a simple question: "Is this going to promote my dreams, goals, and plans?" It is that simple. If you know where you want to arrive when driving, but are not sure how to get there, you follow a GPS. The GPS keeps you on track without taking unnecessary detours. The same could be said for your life in order to achieve your dreams, goals, and plans.

The List Of Things To Avoid Is Very Simple

It was once the way of life that at twenty-one you had access to anything that you should avoid that could derail your future. That age threshold is now much lower, but the concept remains the same. The things to avoid are all related to the seven deadly sins:

Lust: to have an intense desire or need. This is not only sexual, but also anything that overwhelms your day-to-day sensibilities. Do not lust after what others possess or have achieved.

Gluttony: excess in eating and drinking. Too much food, drink (alcoholic, caffeine, sugar-based drinks, etc.) will affect your behavior, ability to function, and move forward.

Greed: excessive or reprehensible acquisitiveness. Your primary focus is gaining more items and wealth for yourself; it is not altruistic.

Laziness: disinclined to activity or exertion; not energetic or vigorous. Waiting for others to provide for you and yours does not promote a life of leadership and growth.

Wrath: intense vengeful anger or indignation. Get control over the potential for irritation in your life. Nothing positive comes from anger. Another word you can use is strife; participating in it will block you from success.

Envy: painful or resentful awareness of an advantage enjoyed by another, joined with a desire to possess the same benefit. Stop looking at what others have done and feeling bad for yourself as a result. Go out instead and do something to achieve for you and yours. Wanting things that others have is not the answer to how to earn it.

Pride: quality or state of being proud; inordinate self-esteem. You may be all-knowing and understanding in your mind. Still, without the action to back up what you think of yourself, you are just living a self-denying lie. This will do nothing but bring about frustration for yourself and most everyone around you.

Walk away from the seven deadly sins and experience a greater lifetime of return on investment.

The previous list details the outcomes of the habits that will derail your dreams, goals, and plans. The first two on the list, lust and gluttony, produce and encourage the remaining five. When you walk away from a life of lust and gluttony, the remaining five are much easier to avoid.

It takes faith and practice to change the habits that led to your personal triggers. Remember to seek support from God and those in your circle of influence. Renewing yourself to God's Word and deciding who on quality in your circle of influence vs. people who just make you feel good, will build the foundation required to make the changes necessary in your life to not self-sabotage.

Summary of Chapter 3

1. Determine what you are doing that keeps you from achieving your calling, vision, and mission. How are you practicing self-sabotage?
2. Whether food (gluttony) or drugs (alcohol, legal drugs, illegal drugs), overindulgence has a zero return on investment, creating emotional highs and lows that distract you physically, mentally, and emotionally.
3. Be kind to everyone always and seek the benefits of peace with all those you encounter.
4. Avoiding the historic Seven Deadly Sins is avoiding self-sabotage.

The wise will inherit glory,
but shame will be the legacy of fools
Proverbs 3:35

Proverbs for Leadership

Chapter 4:
How to Stop Alienating People

Wisdom is principal; therefore, get wisdom.
And with all your getting, get understanding.
Proverbs 4:7

The dreams and goals you have for your life will only happen with the help of other people. Instead of selfishly alienating the people around you, choose instead to help them with their dreams and goals.

Leading A Team

Set your sights on shared goals.

When I was new at one of the jobs I had held during my career, I told the owner I would deliver large contracts. I knew to do that I would need to sell in a way different than I had ever sold previously. To land the whales that I had my sights on, I needed to work with my sales team on a shared goal.

Getting others to stop alienating people is the first rule of teamwork.

The challenge was that the individuals on my team did not like one another or enjoyed each other's company. To make matters more challenging, they sold with different styles. The first sales job that I had to accomplish was convincing them to work together. I needed to get them to stop alienating each other, and even more important, to trust me.

Everyone's leadership style is unique.

I had been assigned to them as their new boss, and they were very comfortable with their old leader. Their former boss was all about defending their lack of production to ownership and making excuses. My style was all about accountability, discovering and removing obstacles, and then putting guards and responsibilities in place to ensure productive days occurred.

Talk to others about their skills you admire.

I saw my opportunity at a sales team dinner that both teams were having together. I purposely had us seated together and began building them up, talking about their skills and how they complemented one another. I continued this strategy beyond the dinner and made it a part of every interaction I had with them as a group and individually.

The ABCs: Attitude Beyond Collaboration

After thirty days of these discussions, I suggested to the team that we needed to work together to land a whale of a sale. They were immediately concerned about territory and who would get the commission. I suggested to them that if we worked on a considerable deal together that individually none of us could ever land, then the commission discussion would go away. This chapter is about the attitude beyond this type of collaboration.

> *"Two are better than one,*
> *because there is a good reward for their labor together."*
> *Ecclesiastes 4:9*

By the way, we did eventually land a deal that increased the company's overall revenue by 12 %. The win was sweet.

Have the right kind of faith.

It is not enough to have the faith to achieve your dreams. You need to have the right kind of faith. Let me explain. You have faith in everything you do. You can have the confidence to succeed, but also an expectation to fail. Think of faith like your answer to the question: Is the glass half full or half empty? Your faith needs to be like looking at the glass half full, not half empty. Faith is not a yes or no response; faith is directional: positive or negative.

Faith is a daily engagement and exercise.

Having faith for your plans, for your level of desired living, for positive things to happen, and for your future in general is something you must work on daily. The farther you get from daily activity to reach your dreams, the less real they become. This results in negative and self-defeating beliefs, which are contrary to achieving your goal.

Forget the past and press forward with expectation to your goals. You need to press ahead, forgetting the less-than-fruitful activities of the past, but having learned lessons from them. Push forward with the plans you have made to reach those dreams.

> *"Do not remember the former things nor consider the things of old.*
> *See, I will do a new thing, now it shall spring forth;*
> *shall you not be aware of it?*
> *I will even make a way in the wilderness, and rivers in the desert."*
> *Isaiah 43:18-19*

Do not concern yourself if what you are doing at the moment is not yielding the results you desire. There is something to be said for simply doing the activity of the moment. Work through your day with the positive expectation kind of faith, not by what you see around you.

Turning Dreams Into Reality

Participate in achieving your dreams.

When others are wasting their time on fruitless pursuits, you need to be participating (notice I do not say working) in your dreams.

> *"For you shall eat the fruit of the labor of your hands; you will be happy, and it shall be well with you." - Psalm 128:2*

The more time you spend participating in achieving your goals, the higher the reality they will come to be. Your mind gives you the ever-pleasing endorphin shot when you work on your dreams. You will thus come to enjoy the journey of activity because you know the outcome ahead.

Assign each day a finish line. As you participate in the achievement of your dreams, it becomes easier to complete those tasks necessary to reach the finish line that you set for yourself. Each day should have a finish line that ultimately leads to the final completion of achieving your dream.

Write it down. Know what you dream of achieving. Set up a plan and write it down. Doing what it takes daily includes the attitude you set for yourself. Write the words down plainly. There is no reason to use flowery language when you write the dreams, visions, and plans for yourself. Review daily the dreams and goals you wrote.

That may sound simple, but let me ask you: What was the last dream you achieved?

Care For Your Community

Focus on helping others.

"What have you done for me lately?" That seems to be the question that so many people ask of others. How about asking instead, "What can I do for you?" Do not focus on what others can do for you; focus instead on what you can do to help others. Be the example of helpfulness, and you will inspire others to want to help you.

> *"Let nothing be done out of strife or conceit, but in humility let each esteem the other better than himself. Let each of you look not only to your own interests, but also to the interests of others."*
> *Philippians 2:3-4*

You cannot do this with the desire to receive help from others. You must have a genuine heart of helpfulness. Call it sowing and reaping (for those with faith); call it karma (for those with another kind of faith); or call it "honey attracts more flies." Whatever you call it, the key to receiving help from others is first to have a heart and mind to help others yourself.

Stop ignoring the needs of others and engage with them instead.

How many times have you seen someone in need and ignored them? I am not talking necessarily about people begging in the street, although they do need help. How about if you help another person who cannot seem to figure out the answer to a problem? Or, the co-worker who knows the answer, but not how to write a plan? What are you doing to help, coach, and encourage others, and show patience along the way? Every interaction you have marks the person with whom you are interacting. How are you marking them? What influence have you left on them?

Put aside your selfishness.

In the past, I would help others in order to show them how smart I thought I was. Talk about being conceited. Indeed, I did not even need to help them to show them how smart I thought I was. They knew that already from my attitude. I like to think that today I help others as a coach, encouraging them to see what is needed to achieve an outcome, showing them the steps required to discover the answer to the issue that is challenging them.

> *"But do not forget to do good and to share.*
> *For with such sacrifices God is well pleased."*
> *Hebrews 13:11*

The way you approach helping others is a direct reflection of how significant you think the other person is. You can try and mask your disdain for others, but it does not work. People always know when you think less of them. Put aside your selfish thoughts and focus on others, including their self-image, their abilities, their desires, and their success.

Make helping other people a personal, repeatable process.

Make the decision today: you are going to help people. Then, tomorrow decide the same thing again. Keep repeating those two steps until the day you die. If you have spent years only thinking about yourself, this will not be a smooth transition. Nothing worthwhile is easy. As simple as it may seem, you will struggle. Decide daily to help others. Your work will get done; it always does. You have a way of making that happen. The time you spend helping others always comes back to you multiplied, but it just does not happen overnight.

The Secret to Personal Peace, Understanding, And Contentment

Do you want your life to work out? More specifically, do you want to achieve your dreams? Do you want more than you have now? I do not mean acquiring just material possessions, but a more productive, fuller life. You can have a life filled with greater peace, understanding, and contentment, yet at the same time characterized by striving for more, if you stop alienating the people around you.

Collaboration is everywhere.

A life without collaboration is that of relying on yourself above all else. It is an existence where only you make the situations in your life work together for a positive outcome. However, with collaboration, all things are possible. Think about a braided rope. How much more reliable is the line with three strands woven together vs. one lone strand twisted for strength. Three strands working together in collaboration will always be more durable than one.

Collaboration is not easy for many people. Collaboration is dying to self. You need to put aside your ever so perfect way of doing things and handling situations to not only work with others, but also listen to what they have to say. Listening is not enough, either. After listening comes consideration and implementation. You may even have to encourage others to finish their thoughts and dovetail into other points of view to make an even stronger long-lasting outcome.

When you work with others and listen to them, struggle with them, conforming to what they have to say, that is when personal transformation occurs. That is when you stop being like the rest of the world and become something much more. That is when you end alienating people in the world, bringing them closer to you, and begin participating in the art of collaboration. Yes, I say "begin", because when you fail to engage others thoughtfully and continuously, you will backslide from what you have achieved back to where you were alienating others.

Inconsistency is the path of least resistance.

Do not beat yourself over inconsistency. Anything worthwhile takes time, and there will be a series of starts and stops until meaningful commitment occurs. Think about what you have accomplished in the past. Did it come easily? Did you jump right in and achieve all your expectations? If so, then good for you! You are superhuman and need a symbol on your chest. The rest of the mere mortals will contend with the learning process where they patiently are kind to themselves as they crawl, walk, and march forward.

Temptation is your adversary.

Do not give in to the temptation of thinking less of yourself and that you are not able to achieve the dreams of your heart. Do not believe that you cannot collaborate with others, and that you will continue to alienate them. This is a learning process that is not common. If it were common, then everyone would be great at it! Be faithful in your attempts to move forward. Be kind to others along the way, even when you struggle and get frustrated.

> *"My brothers, count it all joy when you fall into diverse temptations, knowing that the trying of your faith develops patience. But let patience perfect its work, that you may be perfect and complete, lacking nothing."*
> *James 1:2-4*

Collaboration overcomes challenges.

Frustration is apathy leaving your body. The understanding comes when you do not act out the failure in a negative way, but instead seek the assistance of others to collaborate with rather than alienating them. Seeking aid in collaboration instead of alienating others will allow you to overcome the challenges in your life today and in the future. Be collaborative and begin connecting with people if you want to achieve your dreams.

Proverbs for Leadership

Summary of Chapter 4

1. Talk to others about their skills that you admire.
2. Work with others on a project you all want to achieve instead of fruitless pursuits. This will force you to exercise faith daily, recognize each other's strengths and work strategically.
3. Change your attitude from, "What Have You Done For Me Lately?" to "What Can I Do For You?"
4. Collaboration forces you to put aside selfish attitudes and die to yourself when you connect with others resulting in victory over challenges.

*Keep your heart with all diligence,
for out of it are the issues of life.
Proverbs 4:23*

Chapter 5: Mastering the Power of Listening and Moderation

*"My son, attend to my wisdom,
and bow your ear to my understanding,
that you may regard discretion,
and that your lips may keep knowledge."
Proverbs 5:1-2*

Plans prepared for a team must have the team in mind.

Bringing Your Best Self

Being friendly is a choice.

The other day, I had an opportunity to be friendly, cordial, and moderate or rude, direct, and animated. I chose the former and not the latter. People respond best when they are approached in a manner that mirrors their personal demeanor.

Pursuit and discovery bring wins.

I had been working on pursuing a prospect at the highest levels within an organization. My pursuit was successful, and I had engaged with the decision-maker and discovered that he was responsible for the geography I had contacted him about. Still, he was the right person to engage with over multiple areas.

Use a CRM; it is your friend if you engage with it.

Although all the facts were in my favor, I knew there would be a discussion. Our company uses a Contact Relationship Manager (CRM) to track all interactions with prospects. I searched the CRM and found that no one had connected with the corporate office, and any engagements had been at the local level without any success.

Do not let the unpredictability of others set you off. Our company leadership gave me the go-ahead to pursue all sites and own the relationship. Almost right on cue, my colleague, who should have been engaging, began acting as though he owned the portion within his territory.

Ask questions in a cordial way.

That's the strange thing about salespeople; we all get along well until there is an opportunity to close a sale and a commission is in the air. I prepared myself for the call, taking his perspective into account. I decided to listen and be moderate. My colleague explained his expectation over and over again. I kept asking where were the records of him making contact. He told me that he had been calling on the local level for years. I then pointed out that there had been no action on any of the local sites until the previous week when he left a message for a potential contact, and before then, there had been no contact with anyone in four years.

> *"Ask and it will be given to you; seek and you will find; knock and it will be opened to you. For everyone who asks receives, and he who seeks finds, and to him who knocks, it will be opened."*
> Matthew 7:7-8

Sometimes, kicking the can down the road is best.

He continued to push back, and after thoughtfully listening again, I told him that there was nothing to discuss until the proposal process began. Still, I said that he should let me work on the account since I had pursued the relationship, and he did not. He relented, and we agreed to cross the proposal bridge once it was released.

You only have yourself to blame.

I understand how he felt. If someone had gotten a prospect in my area, I would be upset too. The difference is that I would be upset with myself because I had not done what was needed to make the correct contact.

Meant To Be

All time spent in preparation is worthwhile.

Often, you find yourself in roles unexpectedly. You spent a significant time preparing yourself for a particular job, only to end up at a different destination. Do not let this concern you. The time spent in preparation was not in vain.

> *"Therefore, my beloved brothers, be steadfast, unmovable,*
> *always abounding in the work of the Lord,*
> *knowing that your labor in the Lord is not in vain."*
> *1 Corinthians 15:58*

The skills you learned in preparation will ultimately benefit you in this role. Personal training is the key to success in any endeavor you choose.

> *"Commit your works to the Lord,*
> *and your thoughts will be established."*
> *Proverbs 16:3*

You think you know your destination. You may think that you were supposed to have been employed in a particular career. However, you could have ended up working in an area that would have been unrewarding to you intellectually and financially. What if the field you had prepared to work in was not that where you were genuinely skilled?

The destination you have found yourself at has the potential to be more encouraging and satisfying to you than any others you may have discovered on your own. Be assured that you have qualified for this time of your life and career you are currently experiencing.

"Before I formed you in the womb, I knew you; and before you were born, I sanctified you, and I ordained you a prophet to the nations." – Jeremiah 1:5

Leaning on your experience creates strength.

Your experience has taught you skills that will bring the success you desire. The memory of your experiences and work towards goals will help you during challenging times. Those times will be easier to move through when you lean on the expertise and training that you have built upon as a foundation.

All preparation is positive, even when, in the short term, it appears to be wasted time.

"And above all, taking the shield of faith, with which you will be able to extinguish all the fiery arrows of the evil one."
Ephesians 6:16

You do not know the future. How what you are working on now and the experiences you are currently living through will bring you the strength and knowledge needed to achieve in the future.

Always be preparing.

You can count on this truth: never stop preparing. Prepare each day for the future. The future you face is tomorrow, next week, month, and year, and even further. Preparation is the confirmation of the expectation you have for what has yet to occur. Living in development each day is your way of exhibiting for all to see that you know you have a future and are committed to making it the best prospect available to you. Make your preparation a consistent, constant, characterization of how you live life. Do not let anything that comes up get in your way.

Distractions are there to...well, distract.

Living the life of preparation will mean that you must embrace courage and steadfastness to avoid the distractions life throws at you.

Sean Litvak

"My brothers, count it all joy when you fall into diverse temptations, knowing that the trying of your faith develops patience.

But let patience perfect its work, that you may be perfect and complete, lacking nothing."
James 1:2-4

Those distractions are just that: something said to keep you from growing, improving, and achieving. This is true of even those situations that seem to have an appealing reward. You must ask yourself if that reward is what you are working toward or is it another distraction meant to take you off course from preparing for the greater reward.

A missed opportunity may also be a missed distraction. Realizing all of this may create anxiety due to a perceived missed opportunity. Walk away from that. It is just another distraction. Instead, move forward and prepare for what you know you are supposed to be.

Your perspective is obvious to only you (say that again). The way you choose to look at people and situations is not the only way that matters. Be aware of the perspective of others, and what you can learn from them.

You impact others daily whether you realize it or not. Looking beyond yourself is a learned skill. You are not born with the ability to respect or even consider the viewpoints of others. You are born with the perspective that the world revolves around your needs, wants, and desires. The difficulty you experience throughout or at some point in your life is overcoming the temptation of thinking that you will not be taken care of if you do not take care of yourself.

I have quoted this scripture earlier, but it bears repeating in this context.

"No temptation has taken you except what is common to man. God is faithful, and He will not permit you to be tempted above what you can endure but will with the temptation also make a way to escape, that you may be able to bear it."
1 Corinthians 10:13

Following that mindset brings us to the point of only considering how actions will affect yourself, and not the broader concept of how actions influence those around you.

You are not the center of any universe, even your own. Overcoming this mindset is not necessarily just overcoming greed or narcissistic tendencies. It may also mean overcoming the temptation of considering who will be there to take care of you if you do not take care of yourself. Walking and living in this temptation are akin to living a life without faith, or more appropriately stated, a life without the belief that there is a way to achieve goals without entirely depending on your actions.

Time spent in worry is time wasted. Once you understand and can implement a way of life that is not all about achievement, but instead collaboration, you will experience significant positive changes. This may sound counterintuitive. However, the time spent in fretting about how you are going to make an impact without collaborating with others is a reflection of personal pride, arrogance, and more than anything else, fear! Living such a life where you believe everything that will positively happen to you must come from your own effort is short-sighted.

Your desire to always be correct is actually arrogance. Living this way is a form of passing judgment. You are judging that you know best in every situation, and everyone else is wrong. You are assuming that no one has an idea worth considering, let alone implementing, since you do not respect their perspective. This lack of respect is both arrogant and ignorant.

Your ideas are good, but not always best. Consider this: if you have all the best ideas and ways of doing things, how did the world, let alone the country, survive, grow, and thrive before you were born? Who was there leading before you? Do you consider yourself that once-in-a-lifetime leader that has all the answers? You are not that person. For the record, neither am I.

Put yourself in someone else's perspective. I encourage you to meditate on this realization and be watchful of your conceited attitudes, both privately and publicly. Such attitudes have a habit of sneaking back in when you most think you have overcome them. Put them aside, and instead consider the challenge ahead from the perspective of another: how they see it, approach it, and ultimately solve it. Doing so will allow you to grow in more ways than you realize.

How you respond speaks more than the words you use. How you respond to those who approach life and situations from a different perspective will communicate the level of respect you have for them more than what you actually say.

Stop thinking of others from your own perspective. Although you are communicating what you think of others and the level of respect you have for them, you must understand what is motivating your response. If the response is positive, you have a mature image of your self-worth and ability to interact.

However, if the answer is negative, the question must be asked: is the response about the other person, or is it about how you are viewing yourself? Do you see yourself as inadequate compared to the other person? Are you responding fearfully because you do not have all the answers? No one does. Do not succumb to this path of least resistance. To do so will only allow negative emotions and experiences into your life and that of others.

Listen more; talk less. When responding to others, it is best to always keep in mind a simple physical fact: you have one mouth and two ears. Spend much more time listening rather than speaking. Those of you who know me may find this hypocritical, but if you truly know how much I have to say, then you would be amazed at my self-control at remaining as quiet as I do.

Being quick to listen is also being slow to interrupt. Being quick to listen and slow to respond will keep you from not only saying something wrong or need not be said but will also keep you from saying something that could create strife. *"In the multitude of words sin is not lacking, but he who restrains his lips is wise."* – Proverbs 10:19 time you take to consider what is said, processing the perspective behind the comments, along with the motivations, will pay off when you do respond.

Dying to self is one of the greatest ways to learn. Gaining knowledge of the benefits of being slow to speak without implementing it with the wisdom of listening, processing, and thoughtful responses means sacrificing yourself and the person or group with whom you speak. By portraying yourself in such a way, you will decrease the level of respect others have for you, thus making collaboration more difficult. You are sacrificing others by forcing them to consider erroneous and fallacious arguments that take time and mental fortitude to overcome.

The more you want to be heard, the less value you bring. The more you increase your efforts to be heard just for the sake of being listened to, the higher the chances are that others will roll their eyes or dart glances at one another when you begin to speak. When this occurs, you will be branded a fool rather than the wise person who holds back. Forensic responses with well-thought-out logic and purpose may be less repetitive, but in the end make a more significant positive impression.

Regardless, your insights and answers will produce a response in others, and you have only yourself to credit or blame for what that reply is.

Summary of Chapter 5

1. Regardless of the other person's response, always bring your best self and be friendly.
2. Unpredictability, possessiveness, and proprietary attitudes of others will attempt to break your moderation. Do not let them win.
3. The universe does not revolve around you. You impact others with all your words and actions.
4. Moreso than being a good listener, be quick to listen and slow to interrupt.
5. The more you want to be heard, the less value you bring.

Hear me now, therefore, O children,
and do not depart from the words of my mouth.
Proverbs 5:7

Chapter 6:
Living the Life of Discretion, Transparency, and Moderation

You are snared with the words of your mouth;
you are taken with the words of your mouth."
Proverbs 6:2

You will find yourself far ahead of your peers when you walk in a lifestyle of discretion, transparency, and moderation.

If you have not in the past, that does not mean you cannot change today. Live your life with discretion, transparency, and moderation by living in a way that is without question to many.

Great Leaders Are Mature

Your behavior is a reflection of your self-image.

There is a verse from the Bible that states:

"When I was a child, I spoke as a child,
I understood as a child, and I thought as a child.
But when I became a man, I put away childish things."
1 Corinthians 13:11

This sums up many of the challenges we bring ourselves. How we choose to act and behave as we age says a great deal about how we view ourselves and our place in the world.

Everyone has done some stupid things because of how they viewed themselves. I know this because I have done them myself. I have said the wrong things, hung out with the wrong people and took the wrong advice–all in the name of not being judgmental of others. The truth is we must judge others by their discretion and transparency in how they lead their lives. If I had exercised a greater value of self, I would have had greater discretion and transparency.

You must have a willingness to grow. I firmly believe that maturity is not about age or position in life. Maturity is about self-worth and a willingness to grow. If your self-worth is low or you are unwilling to grow, you will continue to live an undisciplined (anti-discretion) life and a hidden (anti-transparency) life. That which you should not share, you will, and that which you should avoid, you will embrace. I should know; I have done just that in the past.

Discretion comes with age (for many).

There is a balance between transparency and living with walls. Be cautious about how much personal information you share in the workplace. Now, I live a life of keeping more personal items to myself, although I still fail and allow others to see me without walls, that is, until I decide to put some up. It does not matter that I fail in this area occasionally. What matters is that I am aware of it and trying to improve.

To be discreet is to be characterized by keeping your actions to yourself. How you get to that place is a matter of maturity or, sometimes, age. I have met very mature people who are young and very immature people who are old. For most of us, being discreet is something that comes with age.

Actions are a manifestation of the lessons you have learned. Behaving with discretion is desirable, but like anything worthwhile, it is a learned skill. Discretion means being right-minded, dignified, self-controlled, and steady. These attributes are manifested in your actions.

Do not let your passions control you. The passions of your youth need to be bridled.

Sean Litvak

"So, flee youthful desires and pursue righteousness, faith, love, and peace, with those who call on the Lord out of a pure heart."
2 Timothy 2:22

You cannot afford to be characterized as "always giving someone a piece of your mind."

Learn to walk in situational awareness. What you say, how you say it when you say it, and where you say it becomes more critical as you move forward in life. Put aside the immediacy of your response and instead replace it with a moderated experience.

Discretion extends to communication.

Your discretion tempered with moderation will allow you to discover and understand the dangers of being indiscreet when speaking. That moderation only comes from training. Training on how to live a discreet life when communicating can come from role models, books, and faith, but it needs to come from somewhere.

As a general rule, humans are not moderate individuals. Consider your history, for example. Compare your current self with the past to determine your growth. Do you want to be the same person you were in your late teens and twenties? Would you define those times as a period of self-control? Leave the passions of youth behind and replace them with the moderated discretion of maturity. This is an act of the will that is produced by training.

Your circle of influence is imperative.

It is imperative to have a circle of influence that freely speaks into your life. Your circle of influence must promote moderate discretion. Are your friends characterized as self-controlled, submitting to those in authority, and walking in situational awareness? Do they model good works, integrity, and dignity and speak about topics without condemnation but instead praise? Is your circle of influence walking away from the worldly emotionality of youth and turning instead toward discretion and moderation? Choose the life of personal authority, rebuking emotionality, and exhorting moderation. If you do that, you will be on the road to discretion.

Be the example.

Show yourself as an example of good works and dignity. The people who walk in moderate discretion are sober-minded, dignified, self-controlled, steadfast, and consistent.

> *"For we are His workmanship, created in Christ Jesus*
> *for good works, which God prepared beforehand,*
> *so that we should walk in them."*
> *Ephesians 2:10*

Do these words describe you? If not, seek assistance from your circle of influence. If your circle of influence cannot help you, it is most likely time to re-evaluate those within it. These are hard words to process but must be explored if you intend to move ahead in life.

Transparency is not the tell-all of your life. Do not confuse being transparent with telling everyone all there is to say. Transparency is when you live life without hidden motives. I do not know anyone who has lived this way all the time; however, that does not mean you cannot begin living that life today.

Transparency will bring you a promotion. Today is your opportunity to review your past and make the changes needed to live honestly and without regret. When you make personal integrity the hallmark of your relationships, it is noticed by everyone you meet. Indeed, your transparency will be a source of promotion.

Personal confusion is a crutch for some people. Ask yourself: How can you make the changes needed to live a life of more moderated transparency? What have you done in the past that was disingenuous? The answers to such questions are an excellent place to start living a life of greater transparency. Maybe you will not like the answers when you first ask yourself such questions. Personal confusion is often a crutch that people lean on when they do not want to admit the truth to themselves. However, the reality you face will reduce your anxiety as you move forward.

Prepare to make changes.

Are you prepared to make the changes needed to your mind, will, and emotions by not allowing them to be the driving force in your life but instead the quality of your transparent decisions? One way is a catalyst; the other is a result.

You should not admit and communicate every idea you have. Some thoughts are meant for only you. There are some ideas that you should not share with anyone until they have percolated for a while, allowing you to flesh them out. Your outstanding thoughts can become quickly dashed when shared too soon, and too often, with the wrong people.

You are capable of moderation. The moderation and balance between transparency and discretion separates you from excellence and pride in a job well done versus folly and shame. Living this type of moderated life will at first appear to be difficult but know that you can achieve the balance needed.

You can recover from mistakes. Even when you mess up, with the proper humility and moderation, you can re-evaluate the error, find the part that does work, and move forward successfully.

> *"But grow in the grace and knowledge*
> *of our Lord and Savior Jesus Christ.*
> *To Him be glory, both now and forever. Amen."*
> 2 Peter 3:8

Sometimes moving forward is counterintuitive. There will be times when you may have to move forward in a counterintuitive manner. The only bad ideas are those you are afraid to consider. Thinking about an approach does not mean implementing it. The consideration strips away all the potential outcomes in favor of the actual result. That is how you will determine if the idea is worth keeping. Can you move forward with the concept of linking discretion and transparency? If the answer is no, then abandon the idea and move on to the next.

You are a choice away from where you want to be. Living a discreet life will allow you to be transparent. You only need to choose to do so. At first, it will be a daily choice and then a weekly one. Eventually, this choice will be the backbone of all your decisions.

Once this occurs, you will have become knowledgeable in living the moderated life of discretion and transparency.

Summary of Chapter 6

1. Behavior is a reflection of your self-image. Do not let stupid past choices (we have all made them) keep you from changing.
2. Willingness to grow beyond allowing your passions to control you is a measurement of your maturity.
3. The company you keep (your circle of influence) is imperative because of the example they set to you and the example you set to them that is accepted.
4. Change outward does not occur until you make the changes needed in your mind, will, and emotions.
5. Focus on answering the question, "Is this moderation?" until you no longer have to ask yourself.

These six things the LORD hates, yes, seven are an abomination to him:
a proud look, a lying tongue, and hands that shed innocent blood,
a heart that devises wicked imaginations,
feet that are swift in running to mischief,
a false witness who speaks lies,
and he who sows discord among brethren.
Proverbs 6:16-19

Chapter 7:
How to Make Moderation the Choice You Must Choose

My son, keep my words,
and lay up my commandments within you.
Keep my commandments and live,
and my teaching as the apple of your eye.
Proverbs 7:1-2

How you respond to feedback will determine how quickly you grow.

Have you ever had this unpleasant surprise? "Everyone hates working with you." How would you respond to feedback like that? I was in my boss's office, and we discussed various topics. Then he told me that there was one more thing we needed to discuss. He picked up the phone and called his most trusted direct report. Although I had the most responsibility of anyone reporting to him, I was still far from his most trusted direct report.

There is a time to listen and not speak.

The MTDR (most trusted direct report) walked into his office and closed the door. My boss asked the MTDR to tell me what they had been discussing recently. The MTDR began to say to me that all of my direct reports did not like my leadership style and had told him that they would prefer to have a different leader.

Do not let hurt and surprise dictate your response.

That comment hurt and was surprising. I had thought that I had a great relationship with my team. I had made a point to ask for feedback, hear what they had to say, and thank them for all their responses. Then, the MTDR told me that the other leadership team members did not like working with me.

I had a choice at this moment. Do I react or respond? Moderation is always the right attitude. I chose to be moderate in my reply.

Spend more time listening instead of talking.

It cannot be said too often: You were born with one mouth and two ears for a reason! If you genuinely want to grow and not alienate other people, you must spend much more time listening to others than talking. To do otherwise will cause you to become angry, reactionary, and overbearing.

How you react to people is all about your response. Reacting is usually considered a negative. In the best of worlds, you will not react but, instead, be known as someone who responds. The word "react" is traditionally viewed by others as negative, while the word "respond" is considered positive. Most dictionaries define or give examples of the word "react" using the words "anger" or "force."

Avoid creating anger within yourself.

Speaking or behaving reactively creates anger within yourself and others. Instead, your goal should be to respond thoughtfully and peacefully. When you simply react, corrupting talk comes out of your mouth and builds into a mountain of situations that quickly spiral out of control.

> *"Let no unwholesome word proceed out of your mouth, but only that which is good for building up, that it may give grace to the listeners."*
> *Ephesians 4:29*

Giving full vent to this spirit of reaction is foolishness. It may feel good at the time and even feel like the needed thing, but in reality, it only creates increased issues between you and others rather than diffusing them.

In reactionary moments, remember what you want to achieve. Be the wise person who puts away all the reactionary communication of anger, wrath, malice, slander, and monologuing speech.

> *"Let all bitterness, wrath, anger, outbursts, and blasphemies, with all malice, be taken away from you."*
> Ephesians 4:31

Speaking in that way creates bitterness. Ultimately, that is not what you are trying to achieve.

Thoughtful Communication

A monologuing speech is one of the ultimate reactionary moves, but it is one of the weakest forms of communication. Stop now and listen, especially if you are in a challenging conversation. Some may call it strife; others refer to it as passion. Regardless, if you are prone to monologuing (or filibustering), the blame is placed squarely on you. You need to stop this act of aggression, learn instead to listen, and become more forensic in your communication.

Be thoughtful in your responses. Utilizing the monologue method creates passions not used in civil conversation. I am not advocating that you should not speak. You must respond thoughtfully rather than reactionary and argumentative. The former is all about listening, while the latter is about what you think, what you have believed, and how you want to influence others to see things the way you do, regardless of the relationships you may break.

Seek to influence others positively. Breaking the lines of communication does not improve the relationship. It destroys the hope of communication and leaves people in confusion and disarray. What is your desire: to influence or control what others think? How you choose to correspond, respond, or react will significantly impact the outcome and the fulfillment of your desire.

Everything has a purpose, but will it profit you? Everything that you read or hear has a purpose. You will profit from whatever you read and hear if you discern what to apply and what to walk away from. Your approach toward all the information available will determine the profit you experience. All of what you read and hear will teach you, correct you, judge you, and ultimately train you to excel.

Peace, Progress, Growth, or Regression?

Your knowledge of what to consider and implement will come from your desired and expected outcomes. Do you wish to make friends or be productive? Are you more concerned with keeping the peace or making progress? Do you want to grow or regress? None of these are mutually exclusive but thought and decision-making is involved. Define your approach to what others put before you. Your response to the information presented will ultimately create the outcome you experience.

Your approach reveals your desires. Notice that I did not say the *outcome* you desired. What you want can shift from moment to moment, but the result you experience is based on the culmination of all your influences. Your approach will reveal what you desire.

Know when to walk away. That is why you must walk away from everything that is self-serving, short-sighted, envious, slanderous, and riddled with hypocrisy.

> *"Therefore, put away all wickedness, deceit, hypocrisy, envy,*
> *and all evil speaking.*
> *As newborn babies, desire the pure milk of the word,*
> *that by it you may grow,*
> *if it is true that you have experienced that the Lord is good."*
> 1 Peter 2:1-3

These are not the bricks in the road that will lead to the outcome you have set your sights on. This discernment comes with maturity, not merely growing older. The level of sophistication you embrace will fuel your approach. Live like no one else today, working on your plan toward the goals you have set, and eventually, you will be like no one else.

It is time to make decisions. You must put aside your youth's childish ways and be mature. Stop being whipped about by your desires, but instead, drink the potion of thoughtful living. The ideas of others do not challenge contemplative life. Grown-up living seeks out the views of others to gain knowledge that grows into wisdom. Have you made the quality decision to change your approach and leave immature pursuits behind you? Or are you still fascinated with them?

The filling of your life is your decision. How you fill your life from void to outcome is up to you. What you fill it with is decided by your approach. The approach you choose today affects the path you want for tomorrow. Putting off today for tomorrow is much more detrimental than you realize. Although you plan to live to an elderly age, there will be an end. How much time will you spend not working on your plan, not growing, not seeking knowledge, and thus not gaining the wisdom needed to live in the moment today?

Your Approach Makes The Difference

"You shall seek Me and find Me,
when you shall search for Me with all your heart."
Jeremiah 29:13

Here is the truth that may have eluded you up until now: changing your approach creates the enjoyment and fulfillment you have searched to attain. You may not realize it, but it is there. The critical point is whether you know the approach is for you. Ask yourself now: are you satisfied with your current situations and existence for them to remain the same for the balance of your life? Once you discover that the answer is no, that is the moment you will change your approach!

Temptations, like some feelings, are a lie. The temptation you feel is a lie. I have heard it said that feelings lie. Think about the decisions you have made throughout your life. The conclusions based on feelings always turned out poorly compared to the choices you thought out logically. You may say this is not true, but I challenge you to consider the decisions that went well for you.

You may think you made decisions based on feelings, but I am confident that decisions with favorable outcomes were not made based on feelings.

Have a 360-degree perspective.

When responding to feedback, it is crucial to have perspective. You cannot look at everything only from your point of view. You must have and participate in the individual's perspective, providing you with feedback. In short, you need to be the other person's advocate, putting their viewpoint before yours.

Do not get lost and ignore reality.

In the business world, this is the "customer advocate." Too often, you get lost in your feelings about the situation and ignore the other person's reality. It is an easy, natural temptation to have a pity party about how hard things are, but I urge you to stop that now! Run away from that temptation and listen to the perspective of the person providing you feedback.

The emotionally driven you is not an adult.

There are many reasons you do not change your perspective from yourself to others. None of them are reasons you will want to embrace, including the fear of what you might discover. Put on your adult pants and take a big drink of reality: the other person's perspective.

Adjustments come over time with perspective.

You cannot rely on emotion to gain perspective. You must instead be sober-minded and watchful to gain another's perspective. Let me give you an example of how to do this. Think about something that you once struggled to do but is now a strength. How did you make that adjustment?

The change came over time when you altered your perspective and continued to do so. You need to embrace the quality decisions you have made about your dreams, goals, and plans and do whatever is necessary to achieve them.

A changed perspective is a sign of personal growth.

You must change your perspective. If you do not, you will always be the person you are today. Better said, if you had not changed your perspective years ago, you would still be the person you were back then. Some of you are thinking that this would be a good thing. If that is you, I have a surprise that you need to consider: there is still hope! The wrong decisions made in the past can be amended, improved, and even removed if you are willing to change your perspective today.

Always, with humility, investigate the feedback you receive.

> *"The reward for humility and fear of the Lord*
> *is riches and honor and life."*
> *Proverbs 22:4.*

Circling back to my introductory story, I spent the next week talking to each of my direct reports and the other members of the leadership team. I told each of them about the conversation and what I was told. Here comes the punch line: They all said they had not had any conversations with the MTDR and had no idea what I was talking about.

My direct reports told me I had high expectations but was fair. The leadership team members told me that, at one time, I had been difficult, but each said that they noticed the changes in how I operated in my role and was now enjoyable to work with. I am very thankful that I chose moderation in place of reacting to unexpected feedback.

When you choose to respond to others with empathy and compassion, it will have a long-lasting effect on your life. Change your perspective!

Summary of Chapter 7

1. When you encounter an unpleasant surprise, that is the time to moderate yourself, sit back, and listen.
2. Your responses in a challenging discussion will influence others; be a positive influence.
3. Regressing to unmoderated responses is allowing yourself to backslide. Do not give in to that temptation.
4. A change in your perspective is a sign of personal growth.

Listen to me now therefore, O children,
and attend to the words of my mouth:
Proverbs 7:24

Sean Litvak

Chapter 8:
Avoiding Distractions Created by Feedback

*Does not wisdom cry out,
and understanding lift up her voice?
Proverbs 8:1*

There is a delicate balance between allowing yourself to experience feelings and avoid the distractions created by feedback.

The Power Of Feedback

Feedback may appear negative at first.

I have had various experiences with feedback through the years. Initially, I would say that none of them have been positive, but in retrospect, they were life-altering moments that I still remember today.

Finding your kindred spirit should reveal shortcomings in oneself. The first was with an immediate supervisor, the most foul-mouthed individual I had met in years. He pontificated, thought he was always right, spoke loudly, and dropped F-bombs like there was no tomorrow. I liked him personally, although he intimidated me. We had many conversations. One memorable conversation came when he told me that I was the most misunderstood person he had ever met in his career.

He went on to say that he understood me, but most others did not. He said that there was something about the way I expressed myself that intimidated others and made them angry at the same time. This was not the first time I had received this feedback. The difficulty was that he had no coaching or instruction on overcoming this flaw other than "Don't talk too much."

"Thank You For Your Feedback."

Several years later, I found myself in a senior leadership position at another organization, and the topic of feedback came up. It was not specifically about myself, but as a value, we needed to cascade throughout our organization. Our leader spearheading the initiative created a curriculum on the value of feedback: how to ask for it, receive it, and in the end, thank the person giving the feedback.

We were attempting to create a positive culture where every time someone received feedback, you were required to end the interaction by saying, "Thank you for your feedback." At the time, those were some of the most difficult words I ever had to force myself to say. Looking back on those situations in my life, I have come to enjoy and even desire feedback. Next, we will discuss how to do that.

Feedback is multi-layered.

Feedback is a funny thing. You need to listen to it, consider it, process it, and then thoughtfully adjust your strategies and tactics based on it. When you work through all that, sometimes you can get fixated on what was said, reviewing it over and over again, thus creating a mental distraction. How do you process feedback yet not get caught in madness?

> *"The ear that hears the reproof of life abides among the wise. He who refuses instruction despises his own soul, but he who hears reproof gains understanding. The fear of the LORD is the instruction of wisdom, and before honor is humility."*
> Proverbs 15:31-33

The answer lies in how you process your dreams, goals, and plans. Feedback gives you a framework for your plans. The first question is: do you have dreams, goals, and objectives? Are they written down? Have you assigned completion dates to the various steps of the plans? Without written dates, these are just wishes.

Feedback without a touchstone measurement shakes your balance. If you have not taken the needed step of writing down and setting dates for your dreams, goals, and plans when you have to process feedback, it can throw you off-balance and create distractions in your life. Why? How do you measure the input? If you have nothing to compare feedback to other than the thoughts in your head, you are setting yourself up for double-mindedness.

Advance preparation is the best way to process feedback.

Have you prepared yourself to give a defense to anyone who asks why you are moving forward the way you are? Better yet, do *you* know why you are moving forward the way you are? Are you able to explain yourself concisely, gently, and respectfully to those who ask questions, or do you defend, divert, and deny against questions from others?

Fear is a demonic force meant to keep you off-balance. You need to walk in confidence, not fear. Fear is just false evidence appearing real. It will only have any power over you if you have not prepared yourself for the inevitable feedback from others, including those who believe you should behave differently.

On A Mission, Or Wandering?

Those individuals giving you feedback will not understand that you are not conforming to the world but are on a mission to fulfill your dreams, goals, and plans.

> *"Do not be conformed to this world, but be transformed by the renewing of your mind, that you may prove what is the good and acceptable and perfect will of God."*
> Romans 12:2

Here is the vital question: Are you on a mission to achieve your dreams, goals, and plans, or has someone found out that you are just flailing around, simply hoping the actions you are executing will work out?

Writing is the key to much in life, especially feedback. You must have the confidence to overcome possible distractions that the feedback of others can produce. That confidence comes from written and thought-out dreams, goals, and plans. It does not matter if you do not know the complete plan so long as you know enough of it, especially the part you are working on now and the subsequent immediate steps.

Beware of your personal delay tactics. Do not waste time on knowing all the plans to reach your dreams and goals. That, in itself, is a delay tactic to keep you from starting. If I had waited until I knew all the steps involved to write and publish this book, I would still be researching what to do and rather than in the middle of writing it.

You do not need to know everything to win. Do not presume you need to know all the strategies and tactics involved in accomplishing your dreams and goals. Fixating on waiting until you have all the answers is analysis paralysis.

What you prioritize, you fulfill. Prioritize time daily to work on your current plan to fulfill your dreams and goals. Suppose you prioritize the time necessary each day to work on your plan. In that case, when the inevitable feedback comes and causes others to question their tactics, you will not, but instead, adjust to becoming even more efficient.

The words you hear from others, including their feedback, can make you feel anxious. Let me remind you again that feelings lie! Anxiety is a lying feeling. If you allow yourself to be run over by emotions, you will forever question your mental state.

However, what about when you experience (not just "feel") anxiety? There is a difference between feeling and experiencing. The experience of fear means you are alive and have not shut yourself off from the rest of the people on the earth. Enjoy being yourself and know you are alive.

Sean Litvak

Power Over Your Emotions

Guard your heart and mind.

You need to guard your heart and mind against what anxiety can do to you.

> *"Be anxious for nothing, but in everything, by prayer and supplication with gratitude, make your requests known to God and the peace of God, which surpasses all understanding, will protect your hearts and minds through Christ Jesus"*
> Philippians 4:6-7

You must be strong and courageous in the face of stress rather than falling into the pit of emotion. Do you find yourself frightened and dismayed when the feedback you receive from others is critical? Does it cut you to the bone? How do you respond? I hope not in anger. That will only provoke others to release an even greater critical barrage and spirit toward you.

Do whatever is necessary for a moderate response.

Instead, do whatever is necessary not to be overcome by emotion. Be known as someone who is slow-tempered, quiet, and avoids contention. How you respond in feedback periods when feelings attempt to control will illustrate whether you are self-controlled or controlled by others. Who is controlling you? Your emotions and that of others, or your anchor of conviction to your dreams, goals, and the plan to achieve them?

Becoming too emotional when you receive feedback that is not to your liking or is aggressive feeds into the intention of the person giving the attacking feedback. Are you going to be a willing participant giving in to someone else who desires to derail your dreams, goals, and plans?

You have power over yourself. The only person who can give others that ability is you. You have the power to experience joy and self-control in all situations. When faced with a challenge that has the potential to become emotional, walk instead with a joyful heart. Joy is more than happiness. Happiness is a feeling. Joy is the experience of your soul, mind, will, and emotions. If emotions are going to move you, then be in control of your feelings, and do not give them over to others.

Joy creates hope and optimism. When you are joyless, you fixate on the worst-case scenario. You believe that everything you do will not turn out how you desire, and everyone will know how you feel due to your frowning face. With joy, your outlook will be hopeful and optimistic. Your actions will be those of someone who knows, not believes; they cannot fail. The joy you experience in your heart will put a smile on your face, energy to your step, and laughter in your voice.

"Now may the God of hope fill you with all joy and peace in believing, so that you may abound in hope,
through the power of the Holy Spirit."
Romans 15:13

Decide where to direct your feelings. You are going to experience emotion. Therefore, you need to decide where and to what end you will be directing the feelings you experience and then put the steps in place to ensure success.

Feelings lie, but you must allow yourself to experience emotions. There is a difference between experiencing emotions and spiraling into them. When we experience emotions, we must take the time to name them and recognize the thoughts they stir inside us. We run into trouble when we allow negative thoughts to build on each other, sending our moods spiraling.

Develop Roots And Build Strength.

Experiencing life means developing roots and grounding yourself, as opposed to merely feeling things, which subverts roots and grounding. Experiencing life also builds strength and allows you to comprehend it, as opposed to just feeling it, which makes you weak and creates confusion.

Experiencing life brings you wisdom that will grow into understanding and then knowledge. With feelings, however, you rummage over and over about that you have no control over.

Feelings out of control can commiserate. Experiencing allows you to see what is available in the world and spin it into something new and transformational instead of feelings that overwhelm you into commiserating with the masses.

Discern the steps needed. Experience allows you to survive tests and discern the steps needed to move ahead, while feelings are an exercise in looking back in regret and saying "if only" to yourself.

Experience reveals others' mistakes. Experience allows you to take what someone else has learned and make it your own vs. feelings of making mistakes that others have made innumerable times.

Laughing instead of weeping. The feelings will make you weep, while experience will make you laugh. Remember the experience. Feelings are something you want to forget, and experience is something you want to enjoy, relish, and relive. The key is acknowledging the way you feel versus allowing your emotions to control your response

This entire chapter has been about how to respond to and process feedback. You are not a program or an app that can take in data and produce an outcome. You are flesh, and with that comes the experiential response. If you allow yourself to get too caught up in feelings, you will feel remorse, betrayal, anger, and confusion, to name a few.

Instead, allow yourself to experience, hear, and process feedback. This will be the catalyst for growth and familiarity that you and your team desire.

Summary of Chapter 8

1. Feedback can initially appear negative but is multi-layered and helpful.
2. Feedback is best digested after you have heard it, considered it, and processed it. Reacting to it is a waste of time.
3. Understanding the feedback you receive is not for the weak. Do whatever is necessary for a moderate response.
4. Acknowledge the way you feel during feedback instead of allowing your emotions to control your response

*Hear Instruction, and be wise,
and do not refuse it.
Proverbs 8:33*

Chapter 9:
Scrutinizing Feedback and Motivation of Others

"Whoever is simple, let him turn in here."
As for him who wants understanding, she says to him,
"Come, eat of my bread, and drink of the wine which I have mixed.
Forsake foolishness and live, and go in the way of understanding."
Proverbs 9:4-6

Examine the source of feedback and the source's motivations. Awareness of the source's agenda does not mean you should not consider the input.

Trust Develops Over Time - Do Not Allow Yourself To Become Jaded

At one time, I had a very trusting nature. I say "at one time" because although I am considered today by many to trust others to the point of being naive, I was even more trusting in the past. I honestly thought that most people desired to help others. Walking that way, I allowed myself to be taken advantage of multiple times. I should have, could have, allowed myself to become jaded and not trust people. I even went through a very short phase with that attitude but quickly pulled myself out of it.

Although I probably still trust others too quickly, I know no other way of living. Too often, I ignore the source of the feedback and make excuses for the input's critical nature. I tell myself that the other person does not have excellent communication skills.

Be Aware Of The Idea Person Without A Plan

One thing I cannot get over is the type of feedback without a plan. I call this the "idea person complex." I know several people like this and tend not to seek their counsel.

Avoid those with a personal agenda, and be careful of the person giving feedback with a personal agenda. Avoid such people. Sadly, as I can be too trusting, sometimes I miss this red flag also.

Do not depend on your initial understanding. In all situations, you must consider the source of what someone is advocating you do.

*"Remember those who rule over you,
who have proclaimed to you the word of God. Follow their faith, considering the results it has produced in their lives."*
Hebrews 13:7

You need to put aside your emotions and personal feelings about the source of the feedback. Most of all, you cannot depend on your initial understanding of the critique. Your examination of the source of the input is thus paramount to how you process the feedback.

Is the person providing feedback someone you can trust or someone rallying for your failure? If the latter, has the individual changed their opinion and wants to assist you with achieving the goals at hand? Here, you are at a pivotal moment in your historical understanding of the person giving feedback. Approach them with knowledge of the past and expectations of a different future.

Do Not Let Previous Experiences Block Possible Benefits

Without expecting a different future from the source of the feedback, you will not gain the diverse knowledge that leads to new wisdom. Do not let your experience with the source of the input block you from receiving beneficial teaching, reproof, correction, and training. Dismissing what you hear or receive because of your historical experience with the person giving critique is selling both of you short.

Relying only on your historical experience with the source of feedback is not a seed you want to plant, nourish, and grow. Is that the way you want people to treat you? You know there have been situations in your past when someone could look at them and brand you for life, although you have changed since that time. You have made the changes necessary to move ahead and have a new characterization of your life. Allow others to have that same experience when they provide you with feedback.

Your expectations about others will influence and change people, ultimately shaping their viewpoint and how they process knowledge that leads to wisdom. What have you done with the sources of feedback in your interaction? Have you interacted with them in a hopeful way or full of disdain and mistrust? Have you bought into the lie that people do not change? You know that is not the truth when it comes to you, but are you making it a reality when it comes to others?

> *"Heaven and earth will pass away,*
> *but My words will never pass away."*
> *Matthew 24:35*

Are you walking in the conviction of putting aside your past preconceived notions about the source of the feedback? Are you willing to move ahead and give the author of the input the same benefit of the doubt you desire others to provide you? Do you have the personal conviction to make the changes necessary to see everyone as a potential improvement agent for yourself and the team as a whole? What are you doing to communicate that to the many sources of feedback?

Indeed, to accept feedback, you must be willing to put aside your personal experience with those sharing it. Instead, treat them as you desire to be accepted when providing feedback. Just because you have a particular past with the source of the input is not a reason to discard the feedback given!

Constructive Feedback Vs. Critical Feedback

There is a difference between constructive and critical feedback. When you receive feedback, it is essential to put your feelings aside and explore the input before you leap to conclusions about the intentions of the person giving the critique. Is it constructive or just critical? You have heard the term "constructive criticism," that is, criticism that is meant to improve the person on the receiving end.

"Let no unwholesome word proceed out of your mouth, but only that which is good for building up, that it may give grace to the listeners."
Ephesians 4:29

Then, there is ugly criticism. Ugly criticism is not feedback with the intention of improvement. Rather, it is meant to point out errors and areas of weakness without providing an alternative objective or plan of action to improve what is examined. The more productive and challenging goal is providing options for all parties involved to discuss and study.

In a team, employer, or any organization where you are in a leadership role, you are often called on to provide feedback free of emotion or editorializing. Snipping and other personal attacks when discussing issues have no place in any team. You must stick to the facts, whether you are giving or receiving the feedback. Personal attacks, be they out in the open or subtle, are always delivered with an air of criticism.

Speaking ill or evil of someone is the surest way to alienate those involved with your team, including an associated group. Speaking ill of someone is not done with only words but also tone and expression. I have told many colleagues always to have a mirror on their desks and look at it when speaking on the phone so they can see the appearance of their faces. Your expression will show through on the phone, just like when you are in front of someone in person.

Be Warm, Tender, And Endearing

The most productive motivation that must be in place when providing and receiving feedback is sincere affection or, said another way, warmth, tenderness, endearment, and partiality. These are the anti-spirits of criticism. Consider the difference between just telling someone how they messed up and need to fix the issue versus providing words and thoughts from someone who cares and has their best interest at heart and in mind.

Constructive feedback should be delivered with a smile, warmth, a gentle tone, and displaying endearment and partiality to the person on the receiving end. When you speak this way to another person, especially when you are delivering news that has the potential to create strife, you are communicating constructively and building up rather than tearing down.

> *"Have not I commanded you?*
> *Be strong and courageous.*
> *Do not be afraid or dismayed,*
> *for the Lord your God is with you wherever you go."*
> *Joshua 1:9*

Those that know me have heard this before: I have no problem with feedback. Still, I will consider it merely complaining and not feedback if not accompanied by a solution or an effective plan to correct whatever issue is in question. The feedback must be given with at least the beginnings of a plan to correct or improve the situation. Be the creative force of solutions and not the whiny complainer who is excellent at only pointing out what everyone else is doing wrong. Be solutions focused.

Speak To Others In An Honorable And Encouraging Way

Are you going to work together to achieve mutually shared goals or use feedback to put each other down and display how smart you believe yourself to be? I encourage you to have your actions and comments defined by those who look upon them as honorable, just, pure, commendable, and encouraging.

> *"Finally, brothers, whatever things are true, whatever things are honest, whatever things are just, whatever things are pure, whatever things are lovely, whatever things are of good report, if there is any virtue, and if there is any praise, think on these things. Do those things which you have both learned and received, and heard and seen in me, and the God of peace will be with you."*
> *Philippians 4:8-9*

If that is your focus toward the group and you communicate in the way I have discussed, then you will receive glory and praise. If you are as talented as you think, the accolades will come your way, but not at the expense of your teammates.

If you are for your teammates, they will be for you unless they have not learned the lessons of constructive feedback that I have presented. If your teammates act negatively, that is okay. They are revealing themselves as not your teammates and will be removed from the team over time.

Your job is not to focus on the inequity they bring to the table but on the encouragement and solutions you bring. Do that, and you will suffer far less mental and emotional stress because of the trust others will have in you and how you allow yourself to trust them.

Now that you understand how feedback and effective planning intertwine, you need to learn how to respond to those who offer feedback fueled by a personal agenda.

You Reach Shared Goals When You Have Or Allow Many Ideas

Be the person with many plans to present and, through them, produce the desired corrective outcome. Your ability to formulate and present various ideas has the potential to reach shared goals and will distinguish you from your peers. Do not put yourself first in the plans you consider, but instead, the desires and objectives of the team.

Allowing the shared, mutually agreed-upon goals to be your guiding light when formulating corrective plans will set you apart. Everyone has been in the presence of someone who has a personal guiding light. What you present and talk about will reveal your heart. No one wants to work with someone who is inward-facing. Face outward toward assisting in achieving the goals of the group.

You may be asking yourself: "What about me?" I encourage you to be courageous and strong and not to give in to fear and over-the-top considerations of self. Focusing on the needs and achievements of the group has the potential to be frightening. Do not give in to the fear that attempts to overcome you.

Be confident; self-centered and distrustful thoughts are not useful. Such thinking does not have to be your way of living. Instead of leaning headfirst into the negative spiral they produce, turn away from them, and declare to yourself that you have a better idea of how to live and lead.

Plan diligently to be team-focused and support those with whom you work. Working together and not in competition is the way to abundance. What you can achieve alone is insignificant compared to what can be accomplished by the group working in unison. Operating with your agenda and undercutting each other is the surest way to failure.

Those Who Hold Themselves Unaccountable Are Driven By A Personal Agenda

Personal agenda-driven teammates are usually effortless to identify. They are generally not subtle people. They approach giving feedback and life itself with the attitude that their ideas are the only way to success, and, therefore, you must do what they say. They compound this by not holding themselves accountable when their ideas fail. They may say that you implemented the idea incorrectly, or even more blatantly, they will deny what they initially said, which resulted in failure.

Like everyone you come into contact with, these people will teach you lessons you will hold dear for the balance of your life. Consider what they say and do, and glean from it any teaching, correction, and training you can leverage on your team in order to achieve the group goals. Even their wrong ideas and attitudes can be useful for the good of the group.

"But the Counselor, the Holy Spirit, whom the Father will send in My name, will teach you everything and remind you of all that I told you."
John 14:26

Even those with personal agendas may have good ideas, although they may have twisted them to their ends and purpose instead of the group goals. Your job in this situation is to analyze the feedback for portions of truth that will benefit the group. Your agenda-driven teammate will press hard to implement all of their feedback, but do not let them overwhelm you. They may appear smarter, more sophisticated, and experienced, but they are still just a person like you.

The personal agenda-driven person is all about power. They may also be about money and prestige, but ultimately, they are about power and who has it. Their desperation for the power they crave and seek to hold is fueled by insecurity. The personal agenda-driven person is critical and without an effective plan because of fear and their deep-seated insecurity of being found out. Fighting such people just causes them to dig in deeper. You must listen to them twice as much as you speak. In doing so, you will find the areas where you can help them achieve their goals without sacrificing the purposes of the team. The personal agenda-driven person does not have the awareness you have, and that will ultimately be their downfall.

Sean Litvak

The Inexperienced Sometimes Have The Clearest View

"Let no one despise your youth, but be an example to the believers in speech, in conduct, in love, in spirit, in faith, and in purity."
1 Timothy 4:12

Sometimes it takes the inexperienced to look at a situation and ask why not, ignoring the naysayers whose retort is an idea that has been tried before and failed. Some old ideas are attempted at the wrong time or with the wrong people. Thus, do not be afraid to take something old that did not work in the past and make it new again in the present.

Summary of Chapter 9

1. Trust only develops over time if you do not allow yourself to become jaded.
2. Your past experiences with others can keep you from experiencing future benefits with both that person and others.
3. Regardless of whether the feedback you receive is constructive or critical, it is your job to be warm, tender, and endearing to everyone as a characterization (lifestyle).
4. Be aware that those who hold themselves unaccountable are driven by personal agendas.
5. The inexperienced have the potential to surprise you with their clear and uncluttered understanding.

Give instruction to a wise man, and he will be yet wiser;
teach a just man, and he will increase in learning.
Proverbs 9:9

Chapter 10:
Why Thoughtful Consideration of Feedback is Important

The wise in heart will receive commandments,
but a prating fool will fall.
Proverbs 10:8

Without thoughtful consideration of the feedback you receive from others, you will backslide and miss great opportunities to impress.

The Personal Changes You Implement Will Create Different Outcomes

Thus far, I have talked about different situations that have occurred throughout my life. Now, let us talk about the results. When I say results, I am talking in particular about the outcomes that have occurred because I have changed. You will also experience such issues. We all experience various outcomes based on how we have changed our attitude.

In this case, I am talking about feedback. I have found that willing to receive, consider, and discuss feedback will profoundly affect how you perform as you live your life. Additionally, you must remember the feedback you have received and continue to implement it.

Whenever I strayed from the feedback received and lessons learned, I experienced challenges in moving forward. The answer to avoiding these challenges is your willingness to accept, consider, and implement the feedback.

You will not always be giving feedback. There will be many times when you will be on the receiving end of the input. Therefore, it would be best if you prepared yourself to become a good listener.

It's Normal To React Positively And Negatively To Feedback

Understand that the feedback you receive will produce both a positive and an adverse reaction. Some of the feedback will provide you with the knowledge needed to gain wisdom, while other types will appear worthless. You most likely have a preconceived notion of how each of those situations will sound and feel.

Some of the feedback will be beneficial. It will impress, encourage, teach, and be full of knowledge leading to wisdom. This will produce a positive reaction in you. You will also hear disingenuous praise, hollow pandering, and verbal assaults for the sake of creating strife.

As unfavorable of a response as this may be, there is also something very positive about it. When someone provides such feedback to you, they are revealing their true nature. What a gift that is! You now know (on the surface, at least) who is for you and who is not.

Those Who Judge You Are a Gift

*"Let every person be subject to the governing authorities,
for there is no authority except from God,
and those that exist are appointed by God."*
Romans 13:1

Those that speak judgmentally against you just because they can do so are a gift. You will become informed of the individuals who will not fully collaborate with you. A potential future for collaboration is available with everyone, but with some people, that collaboration is further down the road.

Do not avoid any source of feedback. Regardless of who is providing the input, learn from it. Acquire knowledge from the words spoken or gain an understanding of the person speaking. Either way, you are gaining experience that will be useful in life. This includes knowledge of how to act and treat others and understanding what not to do and how not to work. Approach life with the faith that every interaction of feedback is an opportunity to learn.

You do not have it any more difficult than anyone else. You have people placed in your life to encourage you and others that believe it is their place to challenge you because they can. Although I have not been an overly sympathetic person toward these people, I do feel sympathy.

> *"There is no fear in love, but perfect love casts out fear, because fear has to do with punishment. Whoever fears is not perfect in love."*
> *1 John 4:18*

I understand that some people are so insecure in their position that the only way they can feel good about themselves is to constantly tear down others and create strife, chaos, and fear in their teammates. Some of these people are masters at swooping in to save the day from the very mess they have created. Their diversionary tactics are a life lesson in how some work to manipulate situations and people to their end.

It is easy to feel anger and frustration with these people. I encourage you to take pity on them and move on with your life, hopefully helping them change through your example of how to provide feedback.

Feedback Is More Than What It Causes You To Think About

How you consider feedback is about more than the thoughts rummaging around through your head. Your consideration is reflected in what you say, how you speak, your thankfulness, your acting like everyone else, how you let the feedback influence you, and your discernment of how your consideration played out to others.

Your words will be the primary way you communicate the process of considering and processing feedback. What you say will reveal your immediate and processed thoughts to the author of the input. Thoughtfully consider what you are about to say before you speak. Once the words leave your lips, you cannot take them back.

> *"But I say to you that for every idle word that men speak; they will give an account on the Day of Judgment. For by your words, you will be justified, and by your words you will be condemned."*
> Matthew 12:36-37

Almost as necessary, and perhaps more important than what you say, is how you talk. The tone you use when responding to feedback will add texture, traction, and depth to what you say. Your mood will communicate the depth and additional meaning you are attempting to convey, revealing what mere words cannot. The truth of the thoughts you are trying to hide behind flowery and pacifying words will be shown by how you speak the words describing your consideration.

Another way to consider the feedback given to you is to be thankful for it — not just personally, but verbally and genuinely. When you express your thankfulness verbally, you are programming yourself to consider the feedback and not just give it lip service. Those situations and people you are thankful for will occupy your thoughts. Holding back your feelings is another phrase for the word "consideration."

The Gratitude You Express to Others For Their Feedback Sets You Apart

Your physical and mental act of thankfulness is not of the world. It conflicts with the world. Your gratitude for feedback is an active response to not being and acting like everyone else. Your non-conformity in this way will move you toward more significant realizations and successes.

> *"Do not be conformed to this world, but be transformed by the renewing of your mind, that you may prove what is the good and acceptable and perfect will of God."*
> Romans 12:2

Living the life of everyone else by being like everyone else will not produce the results you desire. There is too much mediocrity in the world. If you choose to walk down that path, your future will only be average and standard. Conformity leads to average results. Instead, be transformational.

Allow the feedback to affect you in a way that makes a meaningful difference in your daily life, attitude, and expectations. A significant difference will only occur when you consider the words, style, tone, and timing of the feedback delivered.

Feedback Is Far More Than The Words Spoken

The words themselves are not the sole message. The tone and timing of the feedback communicate a great deal of information. Is the author thankful for the opportunity to deliver the feedback? Does the author have your best interests and future in mind when critiquing you?

You must discern the motivations behind the individual giving the input. Realize that whatever the motives of the person providing it, you have the opportunity to use all the feedback for your good and growth. How and when that occurs is up to you and not the other person!

Feedback elicits more of the same. Once you have received and considered the input, it is necessary to discuss it with the person speaking to ensure you are understanding it correctly and not creating a different narrative in your mind.

Do not be afraid of the feedback and what it means and discuss it to discover further clarity. The fear gripping you will only prohibit fully understanding the input and gleaning from it the wisdom that leads to knowledge and success. Fear of what the feedback means will drive you into situations and conversations that produce negative results.

Viewing Feedback As Punishment Cuts You Off From Wisdom, Understanding, And Knowledge

"But the Lord said to Samuel, "Do not look on his appearance or on the height of his stature, because I have rejected him. For the Lord sees not as man sees. For man looks on the outward appearance, but the Lord looks on the heart."
1 Samuel 16:7

Feedback is not punishment. Do not take feedback as a negative situation. The only sentence related to feedback is ignoring it and avoiding conversations around the topics brought to the surface by it. Ignoring the discussion that will provide wisdom and knowledge is self-inflicted punishment. When you allow yourself to wallow in fear, you are creating self-inflicted pain and driving yourself further away from the success you desire.

Discussing the feedback allows you to gain a clearer understanding of what the author is attempting to communicate and the motivation behind the input. Avoiding the conversation will lead to self-deception 100 percent of the time. Without an explanation, you will lack an understanding of the motivation behind the feedback.

In a vacuum, you will create an interpretation that is the worst possible view as a means of self-protection, thus producing self-inflicted punishment. Instead, it would be best if you discussed the feedback with the person providing it.

Participating in the discussion will lead to fully understanding what the provider is communicating, how it can help you, and what areas you need to improve. Doing this will not only make you a better person and leader but will also allow you to grow in humility. No one enjoys frank conversations, but your willing participation and your positive, insightful response will set you apart.

Summary of Chapter 10

1. Feedback is all about the personal changes you make in how you handle it, creating different outcomes.
2. Feedback, positive, negative, and those that bring judgment, must be thought of as a gift.
3. Expressing gratitude to the person who provides the feedback will not only set you apart from others in their eyes but will also cause you to consider the feedback provided in a more meaningful way.
4. Feedback is not punishment. It is the opportunity to gain wisdom, understanding, and knowledge.

The fear of the Lord prolongs days,
but the years of the wicked will be shortened.
Proverbs 10:27

Chapter 11:
Be Open to People Speaking into Your Life

*A false balance is abomination to the Lord,
but a just weight is His delight.
Proverbs 11:1*

If you think you know where the next pearl of wisdom is coming from, you do not.

You May Come Off As Arrogant Even When You Are Not

Feedback, for the longest time, was difficult for me to accept because those providing it misunderstood my perspective. My desires, dreams, goals, and confidence in my ability to achieve them put people off and made most think I was arrogant. I have had few in my life who understood my position and perspective.

I remember being told by a supervisor that I was one of the most driven, hardworking, persistent, and nicest people who were consistently misunderstood and, thus, made people angry. He went on to say that he had no problems with me because he understood me and what I was driving to achieve.

Another person said that when he asked others about me, he had heard I was divisive and asked me to explain why someone would say that about me. Of course, this individual did not tell me the source of the comment.

What I have learned from these and other encounters is that the wisdom I receive will not always come from the sources I expect, and I need to be open to people speaking into my life. I may not like what I hear, but every bit of feedback has a pearl of wisdom that is helpful to my personal growth. I need to put aside my expectation of self-education as sufficient and instead rely on others' input to grow, even when those individuals have been confrontational to ideas I have presented.

Everyone is not going to be your favorite person. Some people may be those with whom you do not generally want to spend time. The people that are most difficult to spend time with are those that are confrontational with you. The hostility can come in many forms. Nevertheless, you must be willing to accept feedback from them.

When You Are Not Self-Focused, You Will Listen To Almost Anyone

Your willingness to receive feedback from someone who has been historically confrontational to your ideas is a form of dying to self, which means putting your personal preferences aside for the benefit of others or the greater good. When you are willing to die to self, the world opens up to you.

> *"For the one who sows to his own flesh*
> *will from the flesh reap corruption,*
> *but the one who sows to the Spirit*
> *will from the Spirit reap eternal life."*
> *Galatians 6:8*

People will see that you are too self-focused, thus putting your ideas, goals, plans, and motivations first. The life you lead by dying to self will be difficult. However, it does allow you to commit willingly to accepting feedback from everyone, especially those who have been confrontational in the past to your ideas.

Your willingness to accept feedback is not something to be stepped into lightly. You must prepare your mind for the challenges you will experience, including, precisely, the thoughts you will find yourself rummaging through.

"Therefore guard your minds, be sober, and hope to the end for the grace that is to be brought to you at the revelation of Jesus Christ
1 Peter 1:13

It is all too easy to have built expectations based on the experiences of the past. Indeed, that is the origin of most hope. In this case, you must have a different expectation. Expect your willingness to accept feedback to pay off in the long run, thus creating benefits for you and your team and rewards for everyone involved.

Accepting feedback only occurs if you are sober-minded. You need to understand how you have responded to historically confrontational individuals in the past and set your sights on a new and different way of working through situations. You must set yourself to have grace towards those individuals regardless of their response.

Your Willingness To Listen To Feedback Is What Sets You Apart From Most

Grace toward others only occurs when you are willing to be different from everyone else. You need to live like no one else, giving grace to people who have been historically confrontational with your ideas. This way, you can live fully and reap the rewards of the ideas you receive that will create a revelation within you and your team.

Changing how you live will test your mind, resolve, and emotions, but if you are ready, in the end, you will experience what is good, acceptable, and perfect. Nothing worthwhile comes without a price. One of the costs of growth is to display a genuine willingness to listen to all people, process what they have to say, and seek what is worthwhile.

If you are prepared to pay that price, what you receive will ultimately delight you more than you can imagine because it will become a way of life. Dying to the self as a characterization of your life will change you; it will bring you knowledge leading to wisdom.

Do not think about how difficult it will be. Instead, think about the benefit you will receive from your willingness to listen to everyone and hear feedback. The difficulty you feel is in your head. There is no need to talk about how difficult you think it will be. You need to do this without grumbling or arguing. As

> *"Do all things without murmuring and disputing, that you may be blameless and harmless, sons of God, without fault, in the midst of a crooked and perverse generation, in which you shine as lights in the world. Hold forth the word of life that I may rejoice on the day of Christ that I have not run in vain or labored in vain."*
> Philippians 2:14-16

Do not verbalize the challenge if it is in your head and mind. Instead, embrace your ability to move forward, leaving the strife behind.

The Way You Interact With Confrontation Is All About Personal Growth

Who wants to live with strife? The people who have been historically confrontational to you and your ideas are not who you want to emulate, but that does not mean there is nothing you can learn from them. Also, when you allow them to teach you, you have the opportunity to influence them and speak into their lives with how you respond. Think about it. How you reply to such people can change their behavior and help them move forward in a far more friendly and productive way.

Now, look at what is the motivation behind someone being confrontational. Such an individual may not have experienced honor in their lifetime. You need to learn lessons in life. Foundational teaching is honoring other people. This lesson, like others, can be taught verbally through instruction, but a far greater impactful experience is by example. The confrontational people in your life either have not had people honoring them, or they have not accepted themselves.

You cannot expect honorable behavior from someone if they have not seen and experienced it in their own lives. There are so many people hurting in the world who have been mistreated by others emotionally, psychologically, and physically. Imagine the types of lessons people have learned when mistreatment occurs in their everyday life. The harm they have experienced is why you experience hostility from them.

> *"Again, the kingdom of heaven*
> *is like a merchant seeking beautiful pearls."*
> *Matthew 13:45*

What motivates confrontational people is a desire to be correct and respected in their opinion. They are prone to ask more questions than you care to answer and typically want to know why a course of action was chosen. Their questioning occurs because, in the past, they have not been listened to and taken seriously. They have been taken for granted and had their ideas brushed aside, resulting in negative learned behaviors such as aggressively insisting on having their views considered.

Confrontational people may have only experienced hostility instead of gentleness and respect. When someone experiences life having all their ideas questioned aggressively, they learn that is the only way to be taken seriously. Eventually, such people adopt the behavior that has caused them distress.

Your job, if you are bold and strong enough to handle it, is to be a mediator between the confrontational individual and the confronted, even if faced with it yourself. You must approach the confrontational person with gentleness and respect. Make an effort to communicate with them so that they do not need to be aggressive in order to be heard and have their ideas considered.

You can simply push your way through a confrontational person, or you can put forth the effort to help them understand and change. The choice is yours!

Summary of Chapter 11

1. If you cannot accept people speaking into your life, you may come off as arrogant even when you are not.
2. Removing the focus from yourself allows you to listen to others in a greater way, setting you apart from most.
3. An indication of your personal growth is how you handle confrontation.
4. Focus on the benefit of the feedback rather than the difficulty of receiving it.
5. Gentle respect will disarm confrontational people and help them provide the beneficial feedback you desire.

*The fruit of the righteous is a tree of life,
and he who wins souls is wise.
Proverbs 11:30*

Chapter 12:
Energy and Expectation Fuel Achievement

*Whoever loves instruction loves knowledge,
but he who hates reproof is brutish.
Proverbs 12:1*

*Our minds are full of so many ideas, but when you think through them too much,
they become mental roadblocks.*

*Get control of yourself, putting aside the distractions that are keeping you from
achieving your dreams and goals.*

Even Being Friendly And Full Of Energy Has Its Challenges

I remember being full of energy and very talkative as a child. Many who know me today refer to me as the consummate salesperson. It is true that I can easily go into a room and meet many people, engage them in conversation, and generally make a good impression. What people do not know is the mental focus needed for me to be productive with that attitude.

When I was older, my parents told me that, as a child, our doctor wanted to put me on Ritalin or some such drug. For those who are not aware, Ritalin is a drug that is supposed to calm people down and allow them to focus. Nowadays, those taking it and similar drugs have been diagnosed with a condition called Attention Deficit Hyperactive Disorder (ADHD).

Thankfully, at least in my opinion, my parents told the doctors that I was just a boy full of energy, and they would manage and direct me without drugs. Looking back on my life, I see how being full of energy and having high expectations have fueled achievement and success. I cannot even imagine how my life would have turned out if my parents had allowed the doctor to medically moderate me.

Those who experience high levels of energy and have racing minds live a double-edged life of achievement and frustration. They have so much to get done, yet, allowing themselves to be pulled in so many directions creates frustration because they cannot complete what they want or are called on to achieve.

It is like being in a room full of shiny objects and running from one to another without ever realizing the beauty of any of them. Then, you look around the room and become exhausted over what is available without knowing where to start or what to do next.

Have you found that you cannot concentrate, get things done, and be productive, or that you lack motivation? Are you easily distracted? If you answered yes to any of these items, then my response to you is a resounding *no!* You can concentrate, get things done, be productive, and have motivation. You are not easily distracted. What you are is someone who is experiencing mental roadblocks because you are obsessing over what others have not done and how disturbed you are about it.

Excuses Are The Drink Of Many In Society

Yes, I know that sounds like a significant leap, but hear me out. Think about something you have desired to accomplish, but have not. You have every excuse as to why you have not achieved the task, whether it be simple or complex. You are distracted by something you have made a higher priority.

However, distractions and mental roadblocks are the results of wallowing in negativity about something, someone, or situations; and not allowing yourself to be renewed and invigorated to complete the task you desire to achieve or work through. Think about it.

Rather than focusing on the troubles in your path, instead, concentrate on what you can do for others.

"Therefore, my beloved, as you have always obeyed, not only in my presence, but so much more in my absence, work out your own salvation with fear and trembling. For God is the One working in you, both to will and to do His good pleasure. Do all things without murmuring and disputing,"
Philippians 2:12-14

The tasks that you have set your sights on are not just for personal accomplishment but are genuinely for what you can do for others ultimately. Focus on that work to bring peace into your life, as opposed to the challenges that are in your way. When you emphasize the problems, you are keeping yourself from the perfection that is already in place for you. It is yours for the taking so long as you get past the mental roadblocks.

What helps you get past mental roadblocks? The condition of your heart. When you focus on the cares of the world, your heart becomes embittered and bleak with the disappointments you have experienced and the frustrating people you have encountered. Instead, rejoice in the successes, no matter how small or few, and in the joyful people, you have met. Your joyful heart will put a smile on your face and a pep in your step.

"Keep your heart with all diligence, for out of it are the issues of life."
Proverbs 4:23

The other choices are sadness, depression, and anxiety. The anxiety arrives when you desire success but lack results. Put the results aside, and focus instead on how you can encourage and assist others. When that occurs, the adjectives used to describe you will include joy, peace, patience, kindness, and self-control. Who would not want to be thought of that way?

Focus On Helping Others To Remove Mental Roadblocks

When you decide to focus on assisting others, you have done what is needed to remove the anxiety and mental roadblocks that occur daily. Initially, the anxiety and mental roadblocks will decline. Then, this will occur to the point when others may say that anxiety has vanished from you.

However, they do not know you as you know yourself. Do not think you have overcome the fear. Remember, instead of fear, you have focused on helping others and, in doing so, removed the mental roadblocks that slowed you down and kept you from achieving your calling.

Even when you are doing what you think is the right and necessary thing to do, you may still be participating in distractions that keep you from achieving your calling. You thus need to survey the tasks at hand and measure them against the opportunity you have in front of you to participate in pursuits that allow you to walk in your calling.

Do not misunderstand me. I am not telling you to let go and ignore necessary objectives or tasks; rather, you must realize that those essential things will always be there to distract you. Over-focusing on the appropriate goals to be completed prevents you from putting time into the actions needed to achieve your calling.

> *"All Scripture is inspired by God and is profitable for teaching,*
> *for reproof, for correction, and for instruction in righteousness,*
> *that the man of God may be complete,*
> *thoroughly equipped for every good work."*
> 2 Timothy 3:16-17

You must understand that you cannot do everything. You will never make everyone happy. If you attempt to do everything and make everyone happy while not giving yourself the time needed to walk in your calling, you will hate some areas of life. Your mission and the benefits you can achieve from assisting others must be the primary focus of your life.

Now, you may respond, "That's easy for you to say, but I have a job, and it is the primary focus of my life." You are wrong. As I sit here writing these words, I have a full-time job whose focus has nothing to do with my calling. It has been a struggle to overcome the distractions of my career to instead focus on my vocation.

I have learned that I cannot be overly career/job-focused and expect my calling to simply happen. Instead, I must meditate on my calling all day long while accomplishing the tasks, objectives, and results expected by my employer.

I meditate on what I have to do. That is, I look at what I am doing for my employer, pulling away the day-to-day distractions, leveraging the knowledge gained for the benefit of my calling, learning more about myself, and ultimately blessing others. All career situations and goals will be put before you, and you can use the knowledge you have gained for your good. I say: walk away from distractions; instead, focus on how you can help others when you embrace your calling and make it the priority in your life. Do that, and the distractions will disappear.

You Can Run And Hide, But Your Calling Remains

You cannot walk away from your calling. Regardless of the mental roadblocks and distractions attempting to keep you from it, your calling will always be there waiting for you to act upon it. No matter how long it takes you to achieve your calling, the benefits and rewards associated with it will still be there.

"For the gifts and the calling of God are irrevocable"
Romans 11:29

Your calling is the purpose you must fulfill in your life. Achieving and participating in it will restore you. It will confirm the thoughts of grandeur you have had, strengthen you, and establish you like a cornerstone of a building. If all these beautiful things will happen when you achieve your calling, then why do you fight it, ignore it, and choose not to participate in it?

People often choose not to participate in their calling because it takes work, and that is another word for suffering. The suffering you will experience through working in your calling is unlike any other pain you will ever have. On the other hand, the suffering most experience is that of working for someone else.

This includes working for a company, whether it be small or large, a sole proprietorship, a global corporation, or somewhere in between, but always working for someone else for a paycheck. It's about that piece of paper (or, now, direct deposit) into your bank account every other week or weekly that you attempt to stretch far enough to live the life you desire.

Society has grown accustomed to immediate gratification. That is what working for a company is instant gratification. However, the exchange you make for the immediate gratification of income means leaving behind something that is your own.

You are fulfilling the dream and goals of someone else instead of achieving your own aspirations (to say nothing of others in the world you can help along the way) while earning an income for yourself and your family. Yes, you will be receiving an income while working for an employer, but ultimately it is a pittance compared to what you can earn and produce for your family with something that is your own.

With all that said, why do people choose not to suffer? Suffering is viewed by the vast majority of First World residents as double the work. You have worked all day/night for your employer, and now, in your free time, you must work on your calling. Instead, you would rather sit down, watch TV, read a book, gaze at the sky, or whatever it is—anything except put your hand on the plow and turn over the dirt.

You tell yourself how you have worked so hard today (mental roadblock) and how you cannot concentrate on one more thing (psychological barrier).

You would prefer to watch that TV show you like so much (distraction) or finish reading that book (noble, but still a roadblock) instead of taking the time to suffer through the work of turning over the dirt of your calling to plant seeds and reap the eventual harvest for your future.

Embracing Your Calling Eventually Becomes Non-Work

Pressing on to achieve your calling will ultimately award you recognition and all that comes with it, and not just at the end.

> *"Therefore, since we are encompassed with such a great cloud of witnesses, let us also lay aside every weight and the sin that so easily entangles us, and let us run with endurance the race that is set before us."*
> *Hebrews 12:1*

The more you work on your calling, the more you will look forward to the time spent working on it. You will embrace and genuinely understand that you have been chosen for your mission and have the excellence in yourself to reach those lofty dreams and goals.

Achieving them will call you out of the darkness of servitude to another, thus allowing you to provide for yourself, your family, and others in a much more significant manner than you even have been able to envision to this point. It is not just about money. It is about how you can bless others when you remove the mental roadblocks and distractions to achieve your calling.

Decide today to be more diligent, participating in the calling that is within your genetic makeup. Your diligence will pay off over time. It will multiply itself into even more exceptional care, resulting in achieving your mission and walking in peace and expectation.

Summary of Chapter 12

1. Your high level of energy needs to be tempered; otherwise, you run the risk of overwhelming others.
2. Your energy and excitement also have the potential to create personal, mental, and physical distractions.
3. Focus on hearing from God and allowing Him to move your heart instead of you thinking your way through everything.
4. You will not make everyone happy. Remember – Haters are going to hate.
5. Allowing yourself to work on and in your calling will bring you the happiness you desire.

*In the way of righteousness is life,
and in its pathway there is no death.
Proverbs 12:28*

Chapter 13:
Awareness is Balancing Self-Confidence and Admission of Your Flaws

A wise son heeds his father's instruction,
but a scoffer does not listen to rebuke.
Proverbs 13:1

Although you need to be confident in your abilities, you also need to be willing to admit those areas where you are flawed and then do something about it.

Do Not Ignore Your Own Shortcomings.

I confess that striking a balance between self-confidence and admitting your flaws (with the intent to do something about them) is easier to fake than actually embrace. In the past, I have been told that my confidence was offensive and, at times, overbearing to others. Was it a matter of overcompensating for lack of self-image, although I knew I had the capabilities to perform and produce the outcomes desired? Most likely. Still, that does not give me the right to ignore my own shortcomings and act like they did not exist.

There is a fine line to walk between moving forward expecting success and being realistic about your chances of achievement. I had to learn how to keep the confidence needed to execute the role I had earned while at the same time becoming more approachable and not coming off as a narcissist.

Are you in that sweet spot between an approachable and a narcissist? Go ask ten people, and then tell me if you are in that sweet spot.

"So embrace, as the elect of God, holy and beloved, a spirit of mercy, kindness, humbleness of mind, meekness, and longsuffering. Bear with one another and forgive

one another. If anyone has a quarrel against anyone, even as Christ forgave you, so you must do."
Colossians 3:12-13

I learned a long time ago that remaining in that sweet spot is a matter of continually having to admit your flaws, do something about them, and at the same time, not lose confidence.

The way you carry or define yourself is your walk. I heard President George W. Bush once say that in Texas, they do not walk; they swagger. "Some folks look at me and see a certain swagger," said Bush at the Republican National Convention in 2004. Regardless of whether you walk, swagger, or something else, how you are defined is called your walk.

Your walk cannot be defined by what you see but instead by what you believe. Walking only by your experiences is based on the immediate reality instead of the potential future and expectations you have. Focusing on hope for the future will keep you from falling into a ditch because of the challenges of the day.

"Brothers, I do not count myself to have attained, but this one thing I do, forgetting those things which are behind and reaching forward to those things which are ahead, I press toward the goal to the prize of the high calling of God in Christ Jesus."
Philippians 3:13-14

If all you do is act based on your immediate circumstances, then the current temporary situation will likely become your long-term reality. Every moment in your life is fleeting; both the challenges and the encouragements are temporary. Do not focus too much on the temporary things, but instead on how your current situations can springboard you into the future you desire. That expectation is what influences your behavior.

Waiting in patient expectation will strengthen you for the challenges and rewards ahead. Waiting is not necessarily a static state but can also be an active part of your journey. The rest that you receive emotionally from waiting will strengthen you. The patience you gain from waiting for your expectations to manifest physically will illuminate the path you should be taking.

Walking In Your Path Transforms You To Realize Your Potential

The path you walk is a singular one and unlike anyone else's. Walking your path allows you to transform into your single expectation and not conform to what everyone else does. Taking the same road as everyone else will only create a static existence.

On the other hand, allowing yourself to be transformed by your journey refines you toward your potential.

> *"Trust in the Lord with all your heart, and lean not on your own understanding; in all your ways acknowledge Him, and He will direct your paths."*
> *Proverbs 3:5-6*

You are refining yourself through the challenges and tests encountered on your walk. These trials will remove any waste product and leave behind the materials that are the building blocks of the perfection that you are capable of achieving.

> *"The refining pot is for silver and the furnace for gold, but the Lord tries the hearts."*
> *Proverbs 17:3*

You must be willing to leave the love of material things and ways of the world behind and strive forth with the expectancy of what you are capable of achieving. You must not give in to the static existence of the world and the simplistic reality that many are willing to live. You need to renew the excitement and ambition you had in your youth.

> *"Do not be conformed to this world, but be transformed by the renewing of your mind, that you may prove what is the good and acceptable and perfect will of God."*
> *Romans 12:2*

Focus on excitement and ambition as a springboard to what lays ahead. Walk toward the future with enthusiasm and expectation, and do not look back over your shoulder at what you are leaving behind.

When you do that, looking ahead and not behind, you are displaying a willingness to move forward. You are portraying and modeling the desire to all that are watching you and, more importantly, to yourself.

Willingness is more than making a quality decision to take action—that is, a step down the road from where willingness begins. Willingness starts with listening to the voice within you. The quiet voice within you is overshadowed most times by the business of the day and your thoughts. Are you willing to calm yourself and listen to that voice?

Listen To The Voice of God

Some call it your conscience, while others call it the voice of God. I am not going to delve into what or whom that is now. That voice does exist and is speaking to you. The voice will never instruct you to do anything that will harm anyone else. That is a different type of sound. The question is: are you willing to sit back and listen?

Listening, unlike hitting a baseball, for example, is not an immediate action. However, like hitting a baseball, listening is something that requires training. That training can occur on your own but is much more efficient and useful if you are surrounding yourself with a circle of influence that desires to hear the same voice within themselves.

Once you hear the quiet inner voice, however, are you willing to spend more time listening and acting on the steps it is telling you about? Sometimes, the voice will instruct you to do something counterintuitive. The instruction may not make sense from the perspective of how it will be beneficial or move you toward your ultimate goal. Still, it is okay that you do not understand how acting on the instructions will benefit you. If you knew all the answers, then you would not be looking for them.

The more time you spend in the balance between acting on the instructions you receive and listening to the voice, the greater the benefit will be, and the faster you will achieve your goals. Along the way, you will have to face flaws that have held you back. Sometimes, you will have to admit them to others, but most of the time, you must acknowledge your weaknesses of yourself. Once you recognize those shortcomings, you need to make the corrections required to move beyond them.

Moving beyond your flaws will not be easy. You must be willing to look past the errors you made in the past. You must seek others' forgiveness and, more importantly, forgive yourself. Learn from your history, and live a life that does not repeat the same mistakes again and again.

Be All In

You have to be all in. Look forward (and not behind) in attitude, action, and, most importantly, expectation! Are you ready to do that?

The best way to move beyond your flaws is to admit them to yourself and look ahead to a new way of living in the areas that are a challenge. A new way of living means altering your attitude, actions, and expectations. Doing that, however, is always easier said than done.

Making 180-degree changes in your life is a difficult task. You have programmed yourself to act and respond in a certain way to every situation presented to you. That said, you must admit your flaws and make the changes needed. At times, it will feel like you are on the road to destruction, but in reality, you are leaving that road behind and moving forward on the path of freedom.

> *"Is anything too difficult for the Lord? At the appointed time I will return to you, at this time next year, and Sarah will have a son."*
> Genesis 18:14

You must have the faith required to move through the difficult times and on to the more difficult time of admitting your flaws and having the desire, strength, and inner courage to do something about them if you expect to get ahead in life. This process is not about proving to anyone else that you have moved beyond where you were. It is about showing yourself that you can indeed move beyond your past.

To do this, you must have compassion, kindness, and patience for yourself. You must have the humility to understand yourself; change does not occur instantly. You must forgive yourself for taking so long to embrace personal change, ignoring what could have been if you had admitted or come to terms with your flaws sooner. Without that, nothing will occur to drive you in the direction you desire.

You Can Do Nothing Based On Strength Alone.

Your willingness to experience joy, peace, and patience with yourself will produce the gentleness and self-control you desire.

> *"But the fruit of the Spirit is love, joy, peace, patience, gentleness, goodness, faith, meekness, and self-control; against such there is no law."-*
> Galatians 5:22-23

Nothing is stopping you from moving forward other than yourself. You need to see yourself differently now, even when you still have that image of your past self. Leave those images behind.

You can do nothing based on your strengths alone. You have proven that to yourself and others thousand times over. Succeeding due to concentration is something you can boast of. What I am encouraging is moving forward based on counterintuitive action, such as when you have done things that have not resulted in the outcome desired.

You need to trust the still, small voice within to guide and direct you. That voice is not just about action but how to forgive yourself and do something about your flaws. You may not know what to do exactly, but when you sit back, listen, consider the implications of the actions and have faith in the steps, you will move forward.

Stop depending simply on your understanding of situations and life.

"Trust in the Lord with all your heart, and lean not on your own understanding; in all your ways acknowledge Him, and He will direct your paths."
Proverbs 3:5-6

Instead, partner with the still, small voice, and surround yourself with your circle of influence who desire to also listen to the still, small voice within themselves. You will end up having to leave old acquaintances behind if they are holding you back. The outcome you will produce will either encourage your legacy circle of influence or remove them from your life. Either way, it is up to you to decide what you are going to do.

Summary of Chapter 13

1. Be confident, but never ignore your shortcomings. Be humble about them and work to improve. Other people see them and how you respond.
2. Believe the best of yourself in your heart and then put in the work to become that belief.
3. Allow the voice of God, whether it be small and soft or loud and direct, to impact you to change and improve.
4. You can give lip service to others about how you need to change, but God knows what you really believe in your heart.

*Poverty and shame will be to him who refuses instruction,
but he who regards reproof will be honored.
Proverbs 13:18*

Chapter 14:
Your Expectations Are Just for Yourself

*In the mouth of the foolish is a rod of pride,
but the lips of the wise will preserve them.
Proverbs 14:3*

*The expectations you have for yourself are just for yourself.
Others may not live up to them. Surround yourself with a circle of influence
possessing the same drive
without any malice towards those that do not.*

Your Expectations Are Yours Alone

You cannot make anyone into yourself. Well, that is not exactly true. A more accurate statement is that you cannot make anyone who is unwilling to improve. I remember, early in my career, living a life of mediocrity, and I was fine with it. I had found a way to slide by and succeed without really doing much. Although I attended a prestigious (at least in my mind) BIG 10 school, I had no idea what I was getting into.

Throughout high school, I had been an adequate student. I was either in classes that required great commitment and did not do well, or I was in classes for the masses and was bored with how easy they were. You see, I had great expectations for myself, but I did not want to work for them. When I examined it closely, I realized that I had a lack of great expectations.

I did not have tremendous role models in my life when it came to defining and living success. I was loud and talkative, like my father, but not tall and foreboding. I knew I was smart but did not want to do the work.

I entered college, and bad went to worse. With no one to hold me accountable, I got involved with a great yet horrific group of friends. They not only gave me vision and improved personal expectations, but they also assisted me in developing some terrible habits that would keep me from achieving the success I was capable of. I graduated by the skin of my teeth and without a job. As my friends went on European tours for their graduation gifts, I would start a job that I held for two weeks before quitting. Then, I found another job that I held for a couple of months before quitting. A pattern was developing.

I then took a job as a waiter and worked harder than I ever have in my life. I would like to say I made great money, but that was not the case. Somewhere along the journey, though, I knew there was a better way. I knew that I was capable of so much more, and I began to apply myself.

It did not matter what anyone had said to me before that point. I had to make the decision that I wanted more. That is what this chapter is about: having to decide that you want more.

Whether you realize it or not, you live in a world where you must have personal expectations. The question is: what kind of expectations do you have about yourself? Are your expectations encouraging or discouraging? What kind of self-talk is rolling through your head? Do you anticipate the plans laid out for your future are for your welfare or failure? Do you expect a hopeful future? Before you can have expectations of others, you must define them for yourself.

You need to live without anxiety.

"Be anxious for nothing, but in everything, by prayer and supplication with gratitude, make your requests known to God. And the peace of God, which surpasses all understanding, will protect your hearts and minds through Christ Jesus."
Philippians 4:6-7

I know that is easier said than done, but I have evidence for you.

Study the birds and wildlife around you. Do they appear to worry or wring their hands? They are always on the hunt for food and live outdoors. You have a refrigerator and cabinets with food and a roof over your head. Even if your cupboards are almost bare, you still have more saved up than any wildlife creature does.

> *"Look at the birds of the air, for they do not sow, nor do they reap, nor gather into barns. Yet your heavenly Father feeds them.*
> *Are you not much better than they?*
> *Who among you by taking thought can add a cubit to his stature?"*
> *Matthew 6:26-27*

Even when I had less than I do today, I still had a personal expectation for an increase in material wealth. Even with what I have today, I still have hope for expansion. I know that one of my purposes is to increase my wealth. The same is right for you. I come from humble beginnings and understand this perspective.

To many, my family appeared wealthy. Still, money was an issue for us. Do you see my point? Wherever you stand today, there is someone who has less or someone who has more than you. Where you are today does not define where you are going to end up. The defining platform is your expectations.

The Best Personal Expectation Is Moderation

You need to walk without a doubt in your heart that there is greatness ahead for you.

> *"But let him ask in faith, without wavering.*
> *For he who wavers is like a wave of the sea, driven*
> *and tossed with the wind."*
> *James 1:6*

What is that greatness? How is it defined? That is up to you to discover. It may not be what you think it is today. What I thought was true greatness 20 years ago has changed over the last two decades. The more I experienced and overcame challenges, the farther my vision has grown.

At one time, I thought greatness was all about material wealth: both money and things. When I pursued goals just to achieve those things, I found myself walking in an angry, stressed, and me-focused life. When I allowed myself to be content, enjoying what I had, yet striving for more significant expansion in many areas of life, I became far more content, even-keeled, moderate, and, most importantly, friendly.

What I am telling you is not common in the world. The world will advise one extreme or the other. Either make everything all about you and yours, or renounce all worldly wealth, desires, and belongings, focusing only on helping others. I am telling you that both extremes are stressful, and the best personal expectation is moderation in the middle.

Renew your mind, surrounding yourself with a like-minded circle of influence who want to improve themselves and their families while desiring to make a difference in the world.

The drive and ambition you feel and that fuel your life is not for everyone. It can be extremely personally frustrating if you judge others based on how you live your own life. Most of the people you know will likely not be willing to work to the level of success you desire.

Instead of becoming frustrated with them, change your approach. Do not keep asking yourself why so and so is not as driven as you are to achieve. Look inward to understand the reason why some on your team are not motivated to succeed like you: it is because of the way you, yes you, have failed them.

I am saying it is your fault that some of those around you are not achieving the level you have and are not embracing the tools you have provided them to succeed. So, what is a person to do with this realization? Forgive yourself and forgive them. Let that sink in. You are probably asking: "What is there that I need to forgive myself for, and why should I forgive them?"

You need to forgive yourself for not having the patience and forethought to educate, motivate, and encourage others to reach their potential. You need to forgive yourself for the not-so-evident and apparent condescension you have displayed toward others who needed assistance. You have to forgive yourself for giving in to the frustration that you believe others have caused you when it is you that has embraced failure. You need to forgive yourself because somewhere along the way, someone forgave you. You may not have realized it then, but it happened many times. It has happened to all of us.

"For I know the plans that I have for you, says the Lord, plans for peace and not for evil, to give you a future and a hope.
Jeremiah 29:11

You need to forgive others for all the same reasons you must forgive yourself. You need to forgive them for not going beyond what they have achieved in the past and for not believing in themselves enough to do anything different. You must forgive them for only adopting the lessons they learned in their upbringing and not those learned from a circle of influence who desire to see them achieve more in life. You need to forgive them because it is not your place to judge or condemn others. As you judge and condemn others, so too will you be judged and condemned.

Judgment and condemnation only stir up hatred. Hatred leads to strife and moves you further away from your goals, including your desire to assist others.

You have a choice about how you move on after forgiving someone. None are all right, and none are all wrong. The various options are specific to the situation.

Expecting that the other person is capable of change is a positive way to move on. It is the hallmark of trusting that experience can change the individual for the better, and they will learn the lessons of any errors committed. You also have the responsibility of actually trusting the other individual and learning from the mistakes during your interaction with them.

Forgive The Other Person Of Their Offense

Do not be a fool and believe that everything is excellent and all the lessons have been learned. Do not think that you do not have additional lessons to learn. Have you truly forgiven the other person of their offense and learned from the experience, or are you a fool in self-denial, ignoring the warning signs of what lies ahead?

Have lessons been learned on both sides of the offense? How can you be sure? This may seem like an experience that one should never forget. However, you cannot be assured that the other person has learned the lessons without evidence. Only time will tell you the answer to that question, and like all important questions, the response has the potential to change as life moves forward. Admittedly, that is a reasonably cynical statement for such an optimistic stance.

The phrase "forgive and forget" is very encouraging. I would caution that you should forgive the person and forget the offense they committed. However, remember that people can become aggressive at any time; therefore, you should always be on guard.

Still, moving on without expecting the other person to change is a cynical approach. It means you do not trust that the individual has changed for the better and they have not learned the lessons of the errors committed. You, too, are responsible for making sure that the other individual has learned from their mistakes during your interactions with them.

If you think that you do not have additional lessons to learn, then you are as much lying to yourself as you are to the other person. If you do not forgive the other person for their offense and also learn from the experience, then you are a fool in self-denial, ignoring the warning signs of what lies ahead. Without true forgiveness and acknowledgment of lessons learned, you will make the same mistakes repeatedly.

To truly move on, you must forgive the person, forget the offense, and have a positive anticipation of future interactions.

Summary of Chapter 14

1. Do not expect people to live up to the expectation you have for yourself. They can if they want to, but ultimately, your personal expectation is for you alone.
2. The difference between how you have achieved throughout your life and how you want to achieve is all about the decisions you make daily.
3. It is far easier not to worry about the future when you put in the work, and you have faith God has a plan for you, your life, and your family.
4. Forgive yourself for how you have treated yourself and others, and then change, so you do not have to forgive yourself over and over again.
5. Forgive others for whatever transgressions you think they have committed against you. If God can forgive you, you can forgive everyone in your life.

*The king's favor is toward a wise servant,
but his wrath is against him who causes shame
Proverbs 14:35*

Chapter 15:
New is Not Always Better

*A soft answer turns away wrath,
but grievous words stir up anger.
Proverbs 15:1*

*Do not let obstacles, land mines, and time-wasters
turn you and your team from the purpose at hand.*

New Is Not Necessarily Better

"I suggest we do a time study." These were seven simple words that always signaled a trap we had fallen into as a leadership team and that the end of the conversation was at hand without an actual decision being made. Let me explain.

I had the privilege of being on the leadership team of a long-term, well-known company in the industry in which I have served for most of my career. The team was dynamic and filled with passionate leaders about the industry and their roles in the company. At times, the problem was that we were too excited about our positions to the point of doing whatever was necessary to keep the status quo within each of our worlds.

I was the opposite, which was just as challenging, only in a different sense. I was constantly open to new ideas, new systems, and new technology for the sake of always seeking a more efficient way of performing the work that needed accomplishing. However, new is not always better, and trying something new all the time does not create consistency.

Everything Is Not Always Going To Go Your Way

My counterpart was the complete opposite. He rarely wanted to try anything new, and when he did, the test market had to be under his control. My counterpart was all about controlling the outcome. As a group, we would debate various items across our verticals and how they would benefit the company. Inevitably, the conversation would get to the point where my counterpart would say he thought the idea had potential, but there first had to be a time study to ensure the integrity of what we were proposing. Thus, the obstacle went up time and again. Almost every time, the study ended in the proposed idea not being implemented, or it did not occur due to other more pressing items suddenly arising.

Although this frustrated me, I have to admit that my counterpart was consistently the master at getting his way. This chapter is about how to work through obstacles and deal with those that throw them up.

Everything is not always going to go your way. There will be times when it seems as though you are experiencing opposition from everyone and everything. These are the moments of obstacles, walls, and barriers. Fear not, however, as this too shall pass. Your job at such times is to persevere and continue to move forward, regardless of the circumstance or the feelings you are experiencing. Remember: feelings lie.

Meet Obstacles With Joy

You have a choice. Are you going to give in to these boundaries or continue to blaze forward and dig under, leap over, or even burst through them? What happens is all about your attitude. You must meet each trial, barrier, and wall with the best position you can muster. Even more so, the best reaction you desire is to pull the team together. Approach each of those challenges with joy and positive emotions.

What are your alternatives other than having a joyful attitude? Are you going to curl up in the fetal position and have a pity party? Meeting obstacles with joy tells the world that you are not giving in and, even more importantly, that you are not influenced by negative feelings. Instead, you look at obstacles as a test that will produce resoluteness in attitude, action, and expectation. Such a resolution will affect your responses. Train yourself to have the positive hope that leads to a determination of success, thus molding you into perfection, step by step, so you lack nothing.

Make The Hard Choices

Training yourself is great if you live in solitude, but you are a social creature living in the world. It is, therefore, all-important that you choose your friends, associates, and colleagues wisely. You may have some long-term relationships in your life that you need to break. These are the people that create strife and division in your existence. They behave in a way that is contrary to your vision in life.

It may not seem as though they are a hindrance, but you need to be honest with yourself. As you progress, when it comes to people, relationships, and situations, ask yourself if those with whom you are associating are going to encourage or discourage you from reaching your goals.

The answer may be tough to bear. In the end, though, you will experience growth if you are willing to make the hard choices. Have faith that you are making the right decision to move forward, and let that motivate you to embrace the steps needed to overcome the obstacles in your life. The challenges you will face may seem impossible, but when you look back on them from the winner's circle, you will realize that they were not worth the time and effort you are currently putting into them.

Set your mind, not on the things that everyone else considers. Instead, set your mind on where few before you have studied. That is where the answers to overcoming obstacles reside.

"Set your affections on things above, not on things on earth."
Colossians 3:2

Be Sincere And Easily Understood

Your acknowledgment of others and what they have to say is only going to be sincere and easily understood if you have lived a lifestyle of preparation. Living without training is ignorance and will not allow you to grow and succeed. Such laziness will produce a judgment from others that will not work to your benefit.

Your preparedness will separate you from most of the world. Set yourself apart on the front end by being ready for every situation you can imagine. You cannot prepare thoroughly for everything, but you can be somewhat organized. What you do daily is educational, regardless of what you think. You are either educating yourself to lead or follow. There is nothing wrong with either unless you desire one and are achieving the other. Where you end up daily, weekly, yearly, and eventually, it all depends on how you spend your time.

I am not suggesting that you only spend time on self-improvement. On the contrary, there is a place in life for rest and reset. My question is: how much will you spend on downtime? If you say "Every night," then that is the wrong answer. Whether you work to line someone else's pockets (as an employee), run your own business, or live the life of a volunteer, you need to train on preparedness when you are not on the clock. There is always a more significant challenge to face, and you must be ready for it.

Preparation can be incredibly difficult if you have aligned yourself with those who take the opposite approach. Connecting yourself with the unprepared will only drag you down. You cannot pull all the weight in a relationship. Consider the five closest people in your life; you are the average of them. Are the people you see daily encouraging or discouraging you? This consideration is a very sobering moment for some.

If you are attempting to rely on sheer will to move forward in preparedness, then you will fail. Reinforcing and relying on the circle of influence in your life is so important. It is folly to believe that you can be the strong one all the time. You need to surround yourself with a circle of people who will encourage you and pick you up when the need arises. The best circle of influence will do so without you even realizing that you are in need. They will assist you with discernment when you are lacking.

Revisit Your Calling

Looking ahead and preparing for situations that may cross your path is one of the best forms of self-education. You will not be ready for everything now, but if you start immediately and continue, you will move toward a state of preparedness. If you can endure the discipline it takes to move forward in readiness, then you and your team will reap the rewards.

Do not let the travails and challenges of the day keep you from revisiting your calling. There will always be problems to solve. Know when to focus on your mission rather than on the distractions eating away at your time.

If all you do is chase the challenge of the day, then you are forsaking your main purpose.

> *"For I know the thoughts that I think toward you, says the Lord, thoughts of peace and not of evil, to give you a future and a hope."*
> *Jeremiah 29:11*

Whether it is your ambition or that of your team, there are fundamental callings in your life. Spending all your time attempting to correct the issues that present themselves daily will drag you into a never-ending spiral.

You know why you are alive. I have not met anyone who says that their personal calling is to simply chase the challenges of the day, correcting them alone. If that is what you find yourself doing, then you have not trained your team well and are also walking in pride, believing that you are the only person who can correct what needs fixing.

You were each made with a plan to fulfill. If you spend all your time on the activity of the day, you will lose sight of that plan and even grow frustrated because you are not achieving it. The worst part is that it is your fault! Do not lose the vision of your higher calling to pursue interests for the sake of the team. As noble as it sounds, if that is what occupies all your time, then you are running away from your calling. Doing so, you might as well hand over the reins of leadership to another because you have proved yourself unfit to lead. If you cannot work on your calling, then why should you be given the authority to lead others?

Fulfilling your calling will not come quickly or easily. Instead, take back the time you have given away to others and use it for pursuits that you know deep down you are supposed to fulfill. You know your calling, and you understand that it will not be easy to complete. One of the biggest mistakes people make while pursuing their calling, vision, and goals is becoming frustrated when they do not complete them to their satisfaction or quickly enough.

I think back over all the projects I have worked on of any value, and that produced a positive, enjoyable, and exciting outcome. All of them were somewhat difficult and took time. The foundational work required before I could move on to larger projects that produced results was excruciatingly painful and frustrating and took so much longer than I ever would have thought. However, once I calmed down and allowed time to pass, the outcome was excellent. That was always a thing of beauty.

Know that fulfilling your calling will not come quickly or easily. It will be difficult, frustrating, and time-consuming but also enjoyable.

Summary of Chapter 15

1. Sometimes simple words signal a trap.
2. When everything is not going your way, you have to keep your attitude joyful as you meet each trial, barrier, and obstacle.
3. Overcoming obstacles is achieved by a combination of studying past solutions and new solutions.
4. Solely chasing the challenges of the day keeps you from your calling and sends you into a never-ending spiral.
5. If the continual pursuit of "new" keeps you from efficiency and your calling, you are setting yourself up for frustration.

*He who refuses instruction despises his own soul,
but he who hears reproof gains understanding.
Proverbs 15:32*

Chapter 16:
You Only Know What You Know

*All the ways of a man are clean in his own eyes,
But the Lord weighs the spirit.
Proverbs 16:2*

You only know what you know, and that includes who you consider being the potential sources of new ideas.

You Can Only Know What You Know

I have been in the workforce for thirty-five years at the time of writing this book. I have held many jobs over the years but worked for two companies for most of my career. I have worked in telemarketing, inside sales, outside sales, operations, and leadership roles. All these were in the business world.

I have volunteered in associations, led committees, sat on boards, and served in roles that some would not want to participate in as they would appear menial.

Throughout all of these positions, I met a great variety of people, had the opportunity to speak with leaders I would not otherwise have access to, and was privy to several interesting conversations.

All these experiences have revealed to me that the unexpected source is one of the best places to learn about ideas that are worthwhile to study and put in place.

You Cannot Always Rely On Past Experience

I remember picking up one of our leaders at an airport for a meeting. As we were driving to the meeting, he was talking on the phone to one of my colleagues, praising and encouraging him for most of the conversation. Once he hung up the phone, he turned to me and said some unflattering comments about this colleague. My response was a grunt. He asked me, "Why the grunt?" I replied, "I wonder what you say about me when you hang up the phone after praising me." That comment startled him, but I had learned a few lessons.

Never take anything said to you at face value. Consider the person you are speaking with has a personal agenda that supersedes everything else. Finally, look at every experience you have as a learning opportunity to gain wisdom. In this context, there is no such thing as a waste of time.

Everything does not always go the way you think it will. You cannot always rely on past experiences and lessons learned to prepare you for where your next great idea will come from.

Where Should You Look For New Ideas

You may have studied a specific topic, attended lectures about it, and scoured the internet and social media for information just to have someone in the office next to you, down the hall, or across the street bring you the best idea. You may ask how it took so long for this idea to appear and for you to hear it. The answer is simple. You were not ready, and the timing was not in your favor.

You may think that it has taken a great deal of time for a new idea to come your way. However, what if the truth is you were so busy looking in the wrong places (discounting the correct places) that the idea just had not appeared? Looking at the length of your life, how long have you been waiting for new ideas to solve an immediate issue at hand? Was it really that long, or were you simply impatient, seeking instant gratification so you could move on to the next box to check on your list?

The slow speed and delay of new ideas you desire could be due to your lack of creativity on where to find them. I once heard someone say that we cannot cure the challenges of today with ideas and thinking from yesterday. There is great truth in that statement. I would add that we cannot find new ideas and think for tomorrow in the same places we did yesterday. Instead, we need to explore those areas we have not considered as a resource or destination of knowledge and wisdom.

You Need A New Attitude

You need to have a different attitude, focus, and expectation once you discover new ideas and are ready to accept and implement them. You need to be a new creature, not acting like the person you once were, but someone who approaches the challenges of life from a fresh perspective.

> *"Therefore, if any man is in Christ, he is a new creature. Old things have passed away. Look, all things have become new." -*
> 2 Corinthians 5:17

Let the older person pass away, and the new person come out.

If that is the grace you are going to have about yourself, then this is the same grace you should give to everyone else. Give people the benefit of the doubt that there is something great within them. Approach the bearers of new ideas with humility, gentleness, patience, and eagerness to hear, read, and consider what they have to present.

When you approach the bearers of new ideas in this way, they will behave like you are giving them a gift. Think about your response when you receive an award. Is that not the response you want everyone you interact with to have when they work on a project with you? It is all your choice!

The new ideas coming your way should not evoke how you react to the old ideas that have not worked and that someone is attempting to recycle. Do not treat the new plans as though they are dead on arrival. Be open-minded and understand that everyone has a unique perspective, and therefore, you need to give new ideas sufficient consideration.

Your act of giving new ideas sufficient thought is more than just about considering the idea. It is also a type of feedback you are unintentionally giving the author of the new approach. When you provide a new idea enough consideration, you are telling the author of the opinion that you believe in them. You are also looking beyond their faults of the past to consider what they have said and how it has the potential to have a positive impact on the future.

Your ability to embrace even the consideration of new ideas has a monumental impact on their creators. You have the power to either encourage or discourage them. You will either fill the author of the new concept with confidence or dread. You can light up their world and show them the path to further creativity and success. Are you willing to put your ego aside for the few moments it will take to encourage another person to duplicate the progress they have seen in others?

Your Words Will Influence Others

The words you speak to them will make a mark on their mind, their will, and their emotional state. Think about that for a minute. Your words and actions will mark them for a while—either a short time or forever. You thus have the power to influence them to be less or more creative in the future. Every time they consider being creative, they will look to the bank of experiences they have stored up and make a withdrawal.

Behave as if you enjoy inspiring others. If encouraging people does not come naturally to you, that is okay. Pretend it is something you like to do. Read posts, articles, and books on motivating others. Watch videos and follow leaders who are known as encouragers. Your ability to mimic and duplicate the success of others will enable you to produce success in those whom you lead. In this case, fake it until you make it a habit!

You might think that you have arrived at the area of encouraging others when they begin to present their new ideas to you. However, just when you feel you have arrived, the bar will be raised. The bar will continue to increase if you are growing and coming up with new ideas. The seeds you are planting in others to harvest will rub off on you and spur you on to new ideas. It is the principle of sowing and reaping.

Your Prejudices Are An Obstacle

The biggest hurdle you will face when receiving new ideas from unexpected sources is your prejudices against the source. The list of these preconceptions is long: too young; too old; too experienced; not experienced enough; naive; jaded; without influence; too influential; not a thinker; too heady; headstrong; not confident; stoic; flighty.

> *"Let no one despise your youth, but be an example to the believers in speech, in conduct, in love, in spirit, in faith, and purity."*
> *1 Timothy 4:12*

Your prejudice against others for these reasons and more all come down to your opinion of who the perfect source of new ideas should be. Break the mirror and stop looking at yourself. Your bias against others creates turmoil within you and with those around you, resulting in a never-ending cycle of second-guessing. If you had all the answers, there would never be a need for new ideas to enter your circle of influence. Without new ideas, you will quickly become stale and fall behind. You will not be able to keep up with your team, customers, and colleagues. Worse yet, your family will find you also to be outdated. Do not forget everyone, including your family, is an unexpected source of new ideas.

You cannot live simply for the success of today. I am not suggesting you ignore and not enjoy the progress, but the enjoyment must be tempered with continuously moving forward and not resting in the celebration of past achievements. You may be exceptional and gifted, but even the great and talented need new ideas to keep themselves relevant. Those new ideas cannot always come from the same places but must be cultivated and received from unexpected sources.

What have you done today, in the last week, and in the last month to develop relationships with people who will become your next unexpected sources of new ideas? What have you done to thoughtfully prepare yourself for the ultimate unexpected source that shocks you with difficult-to-accept ideas? You may not know what tomorrow will bring, but you do know what you can bring tomorrow. Challenge yourself to interact with one unexpected wellspring of new ideas daily. That same source can be associated more than once if you are engaging about a different topic or situation.

Listen And Let Others Speak

Another hurdle you will have to overcome when seeking to engage with unexpected areas of new ideas is to learn how to keep quiet, listen, and let the source speak. When I say speak, I mean to do so directly into your life. The unexpected source can only speak into your life if you hear what they say without considering how to respond. If you are weighing on how to respond, you might as well be talking over them.

Thinking about how to respond is using the mouth in your head. Instead, hear what the unexpected source is saying and listen to their every word. Treat each word and thought like a pearl found in a freshwater clamshell. Listen to the gleam of excitement when they speak. Visualize the ideas as strung together. Do not think ahead about the potential outcome. Wait for them to provide the information in an uninterrupted setting.

Are you ready for something new? If so, who is the first person you are going to ask to help you?

Sean Litvak

Summary of Chapter 16

1. The unexpected source is one of the best places to learn ideas.
2. Allow yourself to become the new creature that is built on the foundation of approaching the challenges of life from a brand-new perspective.
3. Your ability to consider and discuss new ideas will have a monumental impact on others and yourself.
4. Your prejudice against unexpected sources of new ideas is a hurdle you must overcome to continue building success upon success.
5. Walk in the humility of allowing unexpected sources of new ideas to speak into your life, considering their insight from the outside looking in.

He who handles a matter wisely will find good,
and whoever trusts in the Lord, happy is he.
Proverbs 16:20

Chapter 17:
Become a Productive Teammate

The beginning of strife is as when one lets out water; therefore abandon contention before a quarrel starts.
Proverbs 17:14

As you lead a team over time, the real test of your ability to work in a group setting is when you are not the leader.

How To Become A Productive Teammate

What are the qualifications for being the leader in a group, team, or organization? A great place to start is with the Fruit of the Spirit.

"But the fruit of the Spirit is love, joy, peace, patience, gentleness, goodness, faith, meekness, and self-control; against such there is no law."
Galatians 5:22 – 23.

To me, these also include being:

- Trustworthy
- Inspiring
- Not disgraceful
- Thoughtful
- Self-controlled
- Respectable
- Friendly
- Able to be coached
- Teachable

- Self-disciplined
- Gentle
- Communicative
- Not full of strife

These qualities are a good starting point for some and an endpoint for others. The requirements you need to achieve as a leader are the same qualifications you must perform as a productive teammate. If you never become a productive teammate, then you will never reach the level of leadership you desire. The leader of a group, team, or organization is also a teammate, just like everyone else. What separates leaders from others is the responsibility to ensure the team is moving along in pursuit of its goals. The leader does not perform all the work. If that were the case, then the leader becomes the sole proprietor who does not collaborate with others.

The leader needs to have all those character traits listed and more, whether they are leading or following. Being a kind and agreeable follower is one of the greatest qualities a leader must demonstrate. It is an exercise of humility and displays a willingness to learn. Your quest for self-improvement will be attained when you humble yourself to become the student instead of the teacher. I have heard teachers state that they learned more from their students than their students learned from them. If that is your example, then ask yourself who the student was. The answer is apparent: the humble leader on the quest to gain knowledge in all situations.

When you desire leadership for its own sake, then you are missing the entire point of leading. Leading is a challenge that not everyone can bear. Just because you think you can lead does not mean you can do so. The best leaders have served for years under someone else and are still serving under the leadership of another. Just because you become the leader does not mean you are not part of a team. When you are not leading, you have the opportunity to contribute to someone's leadership. You should not be leading all the time if you desire to grow.

The best and most faithful leaders are those that can put the agenda of others before their own in a meaningful way. It is not always easy, but it does need to happen. When you are willing to help someone else achieve their agenda, you are behaving as a selfless leader.

Learn Lessons From Everyone

Consider every day what your purpose and motivation are in your desire to lead. If the answer is to simply be the boss, then you will fail. You must be able and willing to handle greater responsibilities, the chief of which is the training of others to replace you eventually. Embrace this reality: the more you progress up the leadership ladder, the higher the expectation will be for you to duplicate your abilities and skills in others who will eventually replace you. Your goal should be to coach your teammates to move into your role and exceed your capabilities.

The role of the leader is not something that is handed to you, or at least it should not be. To become a true and successful leader and not one in name only, you must learn the ways of leadership, including the lessons from those who have already succeeded in that role. Here is where it gets interesting.

Who will you allow to speak into your life? In many cases, the student is not the individual making a choice but is simply assigned a leader, coach, or teacher. I have had supervisors in my life who tried to teach me the lessons of leadership, but sadly, many of them were ill-equipped to mentor, let alone lead. I have had supervisors who yelled, were ineffective, were enamored with themselves, and loved to hear themselves talk.

Although some of them were charismatic, they also were deeply insecure, had personal agendas, lied to me regularly, thought the best adjectives were curse words and were intimidated by my skill set and the reasons I was hired. With a list like that, you may wonder how I learned anything from them. In reality, I learned lessons from all of them. The secret is that I learned lessons on both how to lead and how not to lead—the latter being equally important to the former.

I have not forgotten the lessons I have learned. Some would call it experience; I would instead call it life-long learning on comparative forms of leadership. Each of their styles worked to a certain extent in the era they were in at the time. However, most of their methods would not work today. Leadership is not only about learning how to do so but also learning to change with the times. Over the years, the expectation of what is acceptable leadership will fluctuate.

I have had a few immediate supervisors who thought that the best way to lead was loudly, and I do not mean being verbose. These people yelled, screamed, and screeched. It was like they thought they were a parent (and I mean a terrible parent) who believed that the only way to correct their child was to yell at them about what they appeared to have done incorrectly. All the parents reading this will attest that repeatedly yelling at your child does nothing but alienate them, eventually causing them to stop listening and tune you out. The same is true with supervisors who act that way.

All this will hopefully help you understand that there is always something to learn from your supervisors, even those who are seriously flawed. Although it does not sound like it, I would not trade any of my former supervisors and the experiences I learned from each of them. I am happy to say that there is something to be learned from everyone. Do not think that anyone is incapable of teaching you something. They may not be able to educate you in the traditional sense, but they will teach you a lesson you need to learn!

Work With Excellence

I have worked with some highly intelligent and emotionally aware people during every phase of my career, including teammates who were smarter, more driven, and could run circles around me in every facet of my job. I now understand none of that is essential if you do not work with excellence most, if not all, of the time.

The most obvious case of not working well is something incredibly simple: proofreading your work. Without taking the time to proofread, everything that you have done to meet a deadline with the correct data and analysis will fail. Spelling errors, repeated words, incorrect grammar—these are simple mistakes that can be avoided by proofreading, and if not corrected, will keep you from producing quality outcomes.

Youth and a lack of experience can be obstacles to excellence. However, this is an issue that is easy to overcome when you present exceptional work that is increasingly improving. Regardless of your experience, how you handle yourself is paramount.

"Let no one despise your youth, nut be an example to the believers in speech, in conduct, in love, in spirit, in faith, and in purity."
1 Timothy 4:12

When you are inexperienced, manage and introduce yourself as someone who has no reason to be ashamed. Let your work and demeanor speak for themselves. When you are experienced, handle yourself as the elder statesman, always ready to assist in humility and grace. Never behave in an arrogant, aloof manner.

"Do not multiply proud speech, nor let arrogance come out of your mouth, for the Lord is the God of knowledge,
and by him actions are examined."
1 Samuel 2:3

As your career progresses, you will gain experience, responsibility, and perhaps even some prestige. However, do not let this go to your head. What you have now achieved is the reward of being allowed to work on projects of increasing difficulty while at the same time mentoring others to replace you eventually. You have an expiration date in your roles. Do not make the mistake of thinking that your organization cannot move forward without you. As you rise through the ranks, your job is to make sure the organization runs even better once you leave.

None of this is possible if you do not have faith in your abilities. To be clear, I am not talking about arrogance that manifests itself. I am talking about the quiet confidence that people recognize but sometimes cannot put their finger on what it is. Some have told me that I am the most tenacious person they have ever met. Others have also told me that I am the bull willing to run over whoever gets between me and my objective. I prefer the former over the latter, but I still need to get in touch with the bull in myself for balance.

Another facet of working well is realizing that not every objective has an immediate deadline. It is vital to be diligent, but being overly persistent becomes belligerent. Learning the progression of accomplishing a goal is excellent; however, you also need to understand that not everyone moves at your speed, and you should not expect them to do so. If you expect others to complete objectives and projects at your pace, then you will alienate your teammates, thus leading to a whole other group of issues. Your speed is not always the best, so be willing to adjust.

I remember sitting with a senior leadership team training at one of the companies I have worked for in the past. We were a very different team in every way: various backgrounds, experiences, agendas, expectations, education levels, and roles within the organization. The trainer we had invited and paid to train us for a few days asked each of us what we thought was an essential facet of our company. Our answers were self-effacing, thoughtful, humble, and confident. We all missed the answer.

The trainer told us that the most critical facet of our company was our team, the people sitting in that room, and the shared agreed-upon goals of the organization we would build together. Most notably, he explained, none of the individual teams we each led could come before our leadership team in the room if we wanted to succeed. This group of leaders had to be first, above all else. We had each thought that our department was the essential team within the company and the key to our success. We learned that day that only with collaboration between all of us would we succeed.

The trainer explained that we could disagree among ourselves in the room as we worked through goals, plans, and issues, but we had to be unified as one voice when we left the room to lead our separate teams. Any hint of quarrelsomeness or backbiting in the public setting for the sake of the individual departments we led had to end. We needed to support, encourage, and show courtesy to one another publicly.

We also had to make our leadership team meeting the most critical one above all other meetings. We needed to set a schedule far in advance and not miss the meeting. We also needed to rotate the leadership of preparing the agenda for and leading the meeting. We agreed to hold the other members accountable for the commitments they had made. Over the next several meetings, we then set about the business of developing goals and plans for our organization.

Looking back on it, we were on the right track, but we failed. I do not remember who started the process of unraveling everything we had put in motion, but we all had a part in it.

Do Not Focus On Fiefdoms

The first rule we broke was the rotation of leadership and holding other members accountable for their commitments. We decided after our first few planning sessions that one specific person should facilitate all the meetings because this person had done such a great job. That was a huge mistake. This decision diminished the individual's role as a department leader and also created a situation where our less engaged colleagues did not have to lead or even practice preparing to lead the group. We lost out on the opportunity to look at the big picture that affected us all: tearing our eyes away from our fiefdoms.

Focusing on our fiefdoms created selfish ambition, conceit, and delusions of self-importance among our ranks. We each began to look out for our own interests, sidelining and dismissing the importance of others. What we had so easily ignored was the first lesson the trainer had taught us: the team, and not the leader, was what would drive our collective success. Instead, we decided to be a leaders' meeting, fighting to achieve our own departmental goals, claiming to focus on the larger goals, but in reality, putting up smoke screens to divert attention from our failures.

I can only imagine what we could have achieved if we had learned to work well in a team when each of us was not in charge.

Summary of Chapter 17

1. The thirteen skills called the Fruit of the Spirit in the bible is the basic qualification of leadership.
2. The best leaders have served under someone for years before being promoted to leadership and continue to serve under someone in a non-leadership role.
3. There is always something to be learned from those you serve; even those with flaws have something to teach you.
4. You will eventually become the elder statesman (or stateswoman) if you allow your work and demeanor to speak for themselves, always being ready to assist others in humility and grace.
5. Your agenda is not always the most important agenda and may not have a deadline of today for the team.
6. Focusing on fiefdoms and your own interests undermines the collective success of the team.

He who has knowledge spares his words,
and a man of understanding is of an excellent spirit.

Even a fool, when he holds his peace, is counted wise;
and he who shuts his lips is esteemed a man of understanding.
Proverbs 17:27-28

Chapter 18:
Balance Response and Implementation

He who separates himself seeks his own desire;
He seeks and quarrels against all wisdom.
Proverbs 18:1

When you do receive feedback, there is a delicate balance between how you respond and what solution you implement.

How To Balance Feedback With Implementation

Looking back at the stories I told you earlier about when I received feedback about personal change, I chose how to reply to each situation. I could either tell the people providing me with input to "get out of my face" (and other equally unpleasant responses) or respond another way.

I chose the latter approach. I decided to acknowledge their feedback and consider it carefully. I could have just nodded or disagreed and defended myself. I chose the high road and instead responded with thoughtful acknowledgment and consideration. I adjusted my interactions with people based on their feedback.

It was not easy, and I did not enjoy it. I also did not think the feedback I received was 100 percent correct, but that did not stop me from considering what I had been told.

Anyone who has worked with me knows that I have a reasonable opinion of myself and do think I am correct most of the time. Over the years, though, I have learned to temper my presumptions and increase my thoughtfulness.

Once you start receiving feedback, your response to the inevitable questions must be clear and concise. If you simply provide smarmy answers, then you are defeating the feedback interaction you are attempting to cultivate. If you have a history of giving smarmy, inciting answers, it will be difficult for people to take anything you say seriously. The same is true if you are always correcting, leading, and shepherding people. You must allow the team to move forward and make mistakes. Your best efforts to encourage a team member to make a great impression has the potential to backfire if you behave in a controlling manner.

Your job, when responding to feedback, is to become the helper that people desire. People do not want someone that is going to give them all the answers. Instead, they want someone who will listen to them, their ideas, and their insights and then respond clearly and thoughtfully. Your teammates do not want someone who is so self-confident that they always have the correct answer and think they know the best way to handle a situation.

Responding with overzealous self-confidence is arrogance and turns people away from you, resulting in a lack of conversation about the feedback you deeply desire. Feedback is the intersection of ideas where you consider the opinion presented. You do not always have the right of way as the leader. Therefore, do not act arrogantly and without consideration toward others.

Instead, listen with thoughtful consideration and discussion. Responding with an open heart will produce unexpected results. Your response to others must be laced with compassion, warmth, tenderness, and kindness, regardless of whether or not you agree with them. The actual act of providing feedback is a great victory for some teammates.

Balance Introversion With Extroversion

People generally fall into two camps regarding feedback: those who do not give feedback out of fear of making errors and not looking intelligent, and those who give more input than necessary because they have an over-inflated perception of themselves.

However, what you see as fear may be introversion. I know some competent leaders who have little to say in a public setting but are full of insight when in smaller groups or privately. Do not try to change those teammates, but instead, draw them out. The balance between introversion and extroversion is a fine line. The best leaders understand this.

Handling feedback from people with an over-inflated image of themselves is best done by example. If you praise them overabundantly due to their volume of feedback, you are asking for more of the same. Be generous to everyone in praise, but recognize those who speak less in order to draw them out.

Balance your appreciation for those who give a great deal of feedback with praising and encouraging those who do not. This method of response will result in balancing out the time spent with each teammate and the amount of time each of them participates.

Do Not Be Enamored With The Sound Of Your Voice

You are not the same person you once were. How do I know that? It is a matter of how far back you look to make the comparison. When you were a child, you acted and behaved a certain way.

> "When I was a child, I spoke as a child, I understood as a child, and I thought as a child. But when I became a man,
> I put away childish things." -
> 1 Corinthians 13:11

One of the ways that you acted as a child was to acknowledge others when they spoke to you. If, as a child, you rejected others when they spoke to you, then I am confident you had a different life experience from those of us who did obey when spoken to.

As a child, I was very talkative. To those who know me today, this will not be a fresh revelation. My parents told me time and again before walking into social situations to not speak until spoken to. In this way, they were instructing me to remain quiet and only speak in order to acknowledge the person engaging me in conversation.

You need to learn this life lesson deeply. Think about the wisdom of simple words; do not speak unless spoken to. Too many people are enamored by the sound of their voice and their thoughts. As a leader, you could become prone to self-delusion: your ideas are best and cannot be improved. Embracing this thought process is another form of lying to yourself. Behaving this way keeps you from acknowledging what others have to say because you are too self-focused.

Acknowledging what someone else has said to you has multiple effects. First, it lets the person speaking know you heard them and are not ignoring them. Second, it causes you to pause and consider the new information provided or questions posed. Third, it creates the opportunity to think about, learn from, and grow due to someone else's perspective. You have two ears to hear; use them.

You need to return to the ways of your youth when conducting conversations with other people professionally, personally, and academically. Not properly acknowledging what others have said to you will prevent both personal and team growth.

Acknowledging what others have to say is a form of encouragement to the person speaking. Everyone likes their ideas appreciated. No one wants their opinions ignored. Lack of consideration creates ill will, whereas correctly responding creates a sense of importance within the speaker. Denying your talkers will only lead to them denying you in the future, thus cutting off opportunities to learn greater truths in life.

All conversations are opportunities for learning, course correction, and training. Not understanding this basic truth as a way of life is the surest path to a lonely existence. If you only depend on yourself for growth, it will result in narrow-mindedness due to being cut off from the ideas, knowledge, and wisdom of others.

You have received feedback and acknowledged it. Now the time has come to discuss whether to implement the input and, if so, how. Before you move ahead any further, it is vital to realize that the feedback (and your actionable response to it) is intrinsic to your future expectations. How you respond to the input demonstrates your preparedness to defend your position and willingness to change.

As you discuss actionable responses, you must communicate with a spirit of power, love, and self-control, not fear.

> *"For God has not given us the spirit of fear,*
> *but of power, and love, and self-control."*
> *1 Timothy 1:7.*

Your answers must be gentle and respectful, so all those involved will understand the steps that will come next. Do not tell everyone what to do; that is what the world does. You need everyone to discern what is right, acceptable, and perfect to implement the thoughts, processes, and programs that have resulted from the feedback discussion.

> *"I urge you therefore, brothers, by the mercies of God, that you present your bodies as a living sacrifice, holy, and acceptable to God, which is your reasonable service of worship." –*
> *Romans 12:1*

Such transparency is exceptionally counterintuitive to what most people expect in conversation. The majority of people assume an automatic implementation of their plan is the best way to move forward. You must do the exact opposite. Not only should you be transparent, revealing all the information you have at hand, but you must also seek counsel from your team on how to proceed. When you do so, weighing all the options as a group, your ideas cannot fail.

Working transparently and seeking counsel has the potential to create anxiety, but do not let it get a hold of you. Your team has worked together well to this point, and now is another opportunity for an abundant outcome. Write a plan and take it one day at a time. Set quality check-ins like you would with any project plan. Working in this way will clear the clutter and facilitate the type of collaboration that you have earnestly desired.

Collaborating this way will build confidence in your team, thus allowing them to achieve a higher level of trust in one another, resulting in the successful implementation of the agreed-upon feedback. The collaboration includes discussing the many plans presented and then narrowing them down to those that fulfill the agreed-upon purpose. Ideas not implemented at this time are not bad ideas, just those whose time has not come. Opinions come and go. Now, therefore, may not be the time to implement one plan over another.

You and your team will know which season is at hand when you trust in the guidance from one another, based not just on your personal understanding but also on collaboration. With this insight founded on cooperation, you can move confidently and expectantly toward your future!

Summary of Chapter 18

1. Anything but thoughtful responses to feedback defeats the feedback interaction you are attempting to cultivate.
2. People want to interact with those who will listen to them, not overzealous, self-confident individuals who must counter every statement made.
3. Behave in a way that exhibits how you have grown, not as a child who has experienced few life lessons.
4. Acknowledging what another person has said is one of the greatest forms of encouragement to them and communicates a spirit of power, love, and self-control, not fear.
5. Working in transparency and seeking counsel will build confidence in your team and allow a higher level of trust.

The heart of the prudent gets knowledge,
and the ear of the wise seeks knowledge.
Proverbs 18:15

Proverbs for Leadership

Chapter 19:
Self-Confidence is a Double-Edged Sword

*He who gets wisdom loves his own soul;
he who keeps understanding will find good.
Proverbs 19:8*

As much as you think you are the smartest person with the best ideas, the fact is someone knows more than you, and they are not the wrong person when they have a better idea.

Self-confidence Can Be A Double-edged Sword

Having a reasonable opinion of yourself is a double-edged sword. When you know you are right and you are leading the pack, no one can touch you. However, there will come a time when you will meet your match and, perhaps, even your superior.

I cannot tell what year it was, but I can tell you the situation. I arrived at our corporate office for a meeting with all the other field managers. I was feeling good about myself. My region was achieving its goals, my ideas were praised, and I was well-respected within the organization. I was working in both sales and operations and thriving.

A new CEO was recently hired. Looking back at this meeting, I do not even recall the topic discussed, but I suddenly found myself on the wrong end of the conversation.

Whatever I suggested was the opposite of the group consensus and, more importantly, the CEO. We began reviewing our regions' performance publicly, and I was confident I would receive praise, even though I had disagreed with the CEO over some items.

My numbers were high, and I was beating the goal, but we then began to talk about the loss of an account that had occurred in the previous few months. Among the group, we discussed a root cause analysis of sorts, although we were not sophisticated enough to determine what I should have done to save the account.

After some suggestions, I became more defensive and dug my heels in deeper, explaining why I had taken the steps I thought was best to save the account. Each statement explaining what I had done was dissected and analyzed. In the end, the CEO cleared his throat, and everyone looked over at him.

He asked me if, after this long conversation, I knew why the account had been canceled. I again started to defend myself. He stopped me and said very quietly, "You failed."

He said it naturally, but it sounded like a shout to me. After all the hard work and excellent overall performance, he called me a failure in public. I was devastated. The room went silent.

The CEO then began to explain what my problem was. As he spoke, I realized he was not calling me a failure but was describing where I had failed. I learned the difference that day between failure as a noun and as a verb. Actions were the verb; that is what occurred. The person was the noun; that is not what I was.

You must fully understand the next statement first before going any further. You will not always agree with everyone, and someone will most likely still disagree with you. Taking that into consideration, and knowing it to be a truth of life, will significantly reduce the amount of personal anxiety you experience.

Sean Litvak

Disagreement Does Not Mean Strife

The disagreement that occurs between two or more people does not have to end in strife. If each person can have a mature conversation about the area of dispute, then there is an excellent opportunity to gain knowledge and increase your circle of influence and potential friends.

There are many items you should consider when disagreeing with someone. First, think about who is actually in dispute; meaning, are you in conflict with the idea that a person or group is putting forth, or is that person/group disagreeing with you? This is crucial to know because the non-aggressor has no responsibility to acknowledge the disagreeing party, although they should.

Second, if it is you who disagrees with an individual, then accept that it is your responsibility to approach the person privately and explain in plain civil terms why this is so. The conversation should not be fancy or dramatic in nature, nor should it be made in public. If the person is willing to entertain your evidence of disagreement, then you have succeeded in establishing a dialogue.

Third, if the person rejects what you say, you now have to decide whether you should involve others and approach them again. However, understand this: sharing the disagreement with others is a double-edged sword that will inevitably cut both ways. You need to prepare to have your argument explored, dissected, and logic-tested. Are you ready for that experience? This preparation is not for the faint of heart.

What about when someone disagrees with you and is willing to discuss their position? First, be honored that the other person thinks enough of you to risk questioning your idea or decision when it is much easier to simply stab you in the back, talk about you to others, or attempt to diminish your reputation.

Second, be prepared mentally and emotionally to have your idea explored and logic-tested. If you are any kind of leader who has participated in thoughtful preparation, then this should exhilarate you and not put you on the defensive.

Third, do not judge the motivation of the person or group questioning you based on its appearance. Most likely, there is something hidden within their agenda. This will not be immediately obvious but will be discovered over time.

Fourth, regardless of which situation you are in, do your best to always present yourself with truth, integrity, and joy. No one likes a lying, two-faced, and sorrowful person.

Determine True Value In Your Business Relationships

Do you live by the adage, "It is my way or the highway"? Do you like to have things your way all the time? Do you find your ideas and plans always to be the best? Must you still have the last word? If these questions describe you, it is safe to assume that you argue with your colleagues.

You may say that you are a passionate person and, therefore, must fight for what you know is right. Everyone appreciates passion, but at what point does your persistence become overbearing? How many people do you have to alienate before you realize that the idea you so fervently defend is actually selfishness?

You may think it is not selfish to be passionate about what you believe is the best way to accomplish a task. What are you valuing more, though, your relationship with your colleagues or performing tasks? Yes, I know you think if your colleagues would just do their jobs your way, then you can have both. However, if you fail to consider and implement any of your colleagues' ideas, then you are selling yourself, your teammates, and, ultimately, your career short. When you work with a team, you are not the sole proprietor, and that means you must involve others meaningfully.

You cannot let your desire to achieve overwhelm the relationships in your life. If you allow that to happen, you will find yourself as the sole proprietor in every area of your life. No one wants to be alone, regardless of how brilliant and gifted they are.

If you allow your passions to drive everyone away, you will end up surrounded only by people who want to use you to meet their own goals. Talk about the ultimate in sowing and reaping. Think about it. You drive everyone away because you are mostly concerned about achieving your objectives; therefore, the only people who can stand to be around you are those who want to use you to meet their desires.

Do Not Be Like The World

I encourage you to do what may seem counterintuitive. Do not be like the world and only focus on yourself and your way of handling situations. Instead, transform yourself by renewing your mind, helping others, and listening to them.

"Do not be conformed to this world, but be transformed by the renewing of your mind, that you may prove what is the food and acceptable and perfect will of God." – Romans 12:2

Find out what ideas others have and how you can help them achieve what they desire. With this approach, you may even learn something from them.

If you listen to others and encourage and assist them, they will be more likely to bend over backward to work with the team and achieve its goals. Collaborating with others will ultimately be a growth experience for all involved.

Imagine how much more you will accomplish when you are willing to put your pride aside and, instead, listen and help others. This is not easy, and the first time you do it, you may experience anxiety. In the end, however, you will be pleased with the results.

You are not going to get everyone to agree with you. Most people, when pressed, will not agree with your worldview or how you respond to challenges. The good news is that it does not matter what others think.

For a book about understanding yourself in order to have better relationships, this probably does not sound like the most consistent statement. That said, it is still valid. You want to get along with others and build relationships with them. Still, where did you get the false idea that you were going to get along with people simply because of what they think of you and your ideas?

The truth is that you will have challenges in the world, some of which will come from people everywhere. The very same people you desire to build relationships with will inadvertently, and sometimes on purpose, tear you down, thus causing difficult and unexpected situations. This experience will seem like an attempt to take you off your chosen path. With these kinds of friends and colleagues, who needs enemies?

However, with the right attitude, you can overcome anything. It is all a matter of your expectations. Are you going to enable the disagreement of others to knock you off course? Will you give others so easily the power over you that they desire? How will you prevent this from happening? You must have a positive attitude to overcome the inevitable hardships of the world.

Your attitude must not be the same as the person attacking you or getting in your way. You need to view this person as someone you can help develop a different point of view. You need to assist them in becoming agreeable. Look at what others have to say as a chance to grow, not argue.

Do not let others' lousy attitudes affect you or rub off on you. Learn from their disagreement and what you can do to end the strife. Be a peacemaker everywhere and in every situation. Practice making peace. If you choose not to, then all you are doing is creating conflict and contention, which are the very things you wanted to avoid in the beginning.

Sean Litvak

Be the adult in every situation and make peace regardless of the other person or their attitude.

Summary of Chapter 19

1. There are times in life, even when you are leading the pack when you will meet your superior.
2. Learn the difference between the noun failure and the verb failure.
3. Whenever you speak in a group setting, be prepared to have your argument explored, dissected, and logic tested.
4. Do not let your desires to achieve overwhelm the relationships in your life.
5. Although the agreement may sometimes be elusive, embrace getting along with others and building relationships with them.

Hear counsel and receive instruction,
that you may be wise in your latter days.
Proverbs 19:20

Chapter 20:
Encourage Others to Speak

Counsel in the heart of man is like deep water,
But a man of understanding will draw it out.
Proverbs 20:5

The only thing worse than negative feedback
is asking for input and receiving blank stares and silence.

Inspire Discussion During Meetings

I have been in meetings and on conference calls where everyone had an opinion, wanted to speak, and, at times, interrupted one another. Those are the calls and sessions I have always enjoyed: lots of giving and taking back and forth, ideas flowing, and everyone looking positively to the future and what we can accomplish together. But, sadly, this is not the normative experience for most.

As a leader and team member, I had experienced that awkward silence when no one was willing to provide feedback, including answering questions.

During the coronavirus pandemic of 2020, everyone spent a significant amount of time on video conference calls. I, too, participated in many such meetings. Anyone on those calls will tell you that when questions are asked, most people say nothing. I am not sure if it is fear of giving a wrong answer, not liking their voice, or some other reason. For those reasons and many more, however, I found myself speaking an excessive amount of time during group video calls.

It even got to the point of being funny on some calls. On more than one occasion, I told those assembled that I would be happy to be quiet and let others speak if they would just say something. I even called on people to answer questions asked by others simply to get the conversation flowing.

Create An Atmosphere For Voicing Opinions

You have finally gotten to the point in your career where you are leading a team. Part of your leadership cadence is a weekly team conference call necessitated by many members of the group working remotely. You develop a plan that includes not only presenting information to the team but the expectation of dialogue.

After your presentation, you then ask everyone for their comments. The response is silence. You then ask, "Does anyone have any thoughts on what we just went over?" Again, silence. The call ends a short time later, and you are dismayed over why your team does not speak up when the opportunity arises.

Does this sound familiar? I am sure you are wondering what to do and how to overcome this all-too-common situation. Here is where it gets interesting.

Have you created an atmosphere where people find it safe to voice their opinions and thoughts and where they will be heard, taken seriously, and have influence? If your answer is, "I think so," you truly have not.

Your team needs to have confidence that anything said or asked will be heard and acted upon by you. Creating such an environment will generate a shared knowledge base that will improve and increase the wisdom of everyone involved.

Facilitate The Sharing Of Ideas

Your passion as a proponent of this shared knowledge and wisdom will be contagious. However, this means not simply sharing what you know but facilitating the sharing among others. For this to occur fully, there needs to be familiarity and more meaningful relationships between everyone involved.

The most successful teams I have participated in are those where we worked hard toward communicating shared goals and where we were even social with one another after-hours occasionally. Clear, transparent communication is crucial to the success of any team. If the organization does not understand its goals and plans, how can it succeed or be held accountable if they fail?

Holding information back and only presenting it in drips and drabs when you see fit will not produce a generous free flow of interaction between you and your teammates. Why should your coworkers give you their precious thoughts, knowledge, and wisdom if you are holding back from them consistently?

Develop Connections Between Teammates

If you desire real feedback, then relationships must develop between you and each of your teammates, along with connections between each of them. The best teams do not wait for the leader to set the plan to meet their goals. In such environments, the team members themselves so enjoyed what they were doing that they created a responsive dynamic amongst themselves to reach their goals.

Your job as the leader is to create a workspace for the free exchange of knowledge, ideas, and wisdom that is free of judgment and creates encouragement. This workspace must be based on the relationships developed between you and all your teammates.

> *"If we would judge ourselves, we would not be judged."*
> *1 Corinthians 11:31*

Another critical part of your job when facilitating a workspace for the free exchange of ideas is removing obstacles. You need to embrace removing barriers and make it part of your daily routine. Your steadfastness in this endeavor will pay off over time.

Removing the opportunity for frustration and identifying obstacles to overcome is paramount for success. The trials you face in identifying and eliminating barriers will test your faith and could cause you to question your abilities. Doubting your strengths, though, is not a bad thing. Facing such challenges will produce steadfastness and, over time, will grow the skills of all involved.

Anticipate Conflict Between Coworkers

The most common obstacles that block feedback are teammates who may create and cause strife and divisions within the team. Counterintuitively, listen to those same people; they should have insight into the balance of the organization. Understand; I am not suggesting that strife-producing, division-loving individuals should be encouraged.

Measure what they are saying and implying for merit. Some people may rub you the wrong way, but they can discern the real issues. Your task is to determine if the individual in question has insight or enjoys creating chaos to shake things up, and so becoming the hero with the answers.

Be Patient With Everyone

Your patience, or lack thereof, can also be an obstacle for the team. How many times have you listened to another person and thought, "I wish they would get to the point. I could explain what they are trying to say so much more efficiently than they are." Be patient with everyone, and you will see your leadership strengths grow. No one wants to follow someone impatient or, even worse, a bully who cannot see beyond their vision, ideas, and plans.

> "I, therefore, the prisoner of the Lord, exhort you to walk in a manner worthy of the calling which you were called. With all humility, meekness, and patience, bearing with one another in love, be eager to keep the unity of the Spirit in the bond of peace."
> Ephesians 4:1-3

Behaving with the strength described will produce character, and your teammates will thus promote your reputation. You can expect to be known as the individual and team that listens and encourages feedback and which produces the best results. You and your teammates will be the shining symbol of excellence in your organization or industry.

Do Not Shame Others

Rather than shaming individuals over their inadequacies, show your team that you desire the best results, career, future, and quality of life for everyone. The finding comes about because you first decided to embrace patience and modeled that approach for your team.

Are you ready to make the changes needed to remove obstacles from your team that will benefit all involved? The steps and change of perspective required may seem daunting now, but compare them to the alternative: continuing the way you have in the past. Which method will produce the results you desire?

Feedback Is A Structured Conversation

Feedback is not just one-way communication; it is a structured conversation that begins as one-way communication. The discussion starts with asking for feedback. That question is presented in various forms: asking people what they think, what their insights are, how they believe your solutions will work, and anything in between. Then, you shut up. To continue talking defeats the entire purpose of requesting feedback.

The purpose of feedback is to explore the situation or process in question. You are examining and improving upon the original presentation. Do not look for praise or platitudes to puff up your ego and personal feelings of self-worth. If that is all your team is willing to provide, they are feeding your conceit and not providing any further understanding.

Your desire to receive feedback will produce a higher level of understanding, diminish controversy and quarrels, and produce a more exceptional outcome than was initially proposed. The objective is not to receive feedback that everything is lovely. If that is all you are hearing, then you have not created a place where your teammates experience the freedom and comfort to respond honestly.

Embrace The Conversational Process

Once you hear the feedback, it is up to you to facilitate conversations to improve. Do you have the stomach for that? Some people will not be kind in their critiques, thus producing great inner turmoil. Others will be sloppy in their communication, providing feedback that is difficult to understand.

However, labeling the feedback as envious, dissension, slanderous, suspicious, and friction-filled is selling yourself and the person providing it short. Whether you agree with the feedback or not, there is a lesson for you.

Embrace the process of conversation. Learn to find value in received feedback.

Summary of Chapter 20

1. If you intend to lead others, you must learn how to draw out people into conversation and engagement.
2. When people experience an atmosphere of safety, they will voice their opinions and thoughts.
3. The safe atmosphere you create will be foundational to relationships between teammates and facilitate the free exchanges of knowledge, ideas, and wisdom.
4. As the leader, you must genuinely embrace and exhibit patience and not even think, "I wish they would get to the point." You may think you are hiding that attitude. You are not.
5. Creating a safe atmosphere where conversation and engagement occur means you will also be on the receiving end of feedback. You will have the opportunity to be offended. Have the stomach to gain understanding and move forward with improvements that were not your idea.

*The spirit of man is the candle of the Lord,
searching all the inward parts of the heart.
Proverbs 20:27*

Chapter 21:
Listen More

Every way of a man is right in his own eyes,
But the Lord weighs the hearts.
Proverbs 21:2

It is an old adage, but the truth remains:
You have been given one mouth and two ears.

Make a point to listen more!

Make A Point To Listen Harder

I need to remind myself of this consistently. At times, I have become so expectant of people not talking that I ramble on and even interrupt others in order to introduce them to all the great ideas I have.

I was marked deeply one day by something a member of the team I led told me. When I asked him why he did not speak more or engage with everyone in conversation, he responded that he did not think we would listen to him even though he knew his ideas produced results.

This teammate ran a tight organization for our company. He could outwork most, if not all, of the management team. He knew how to motivate and lead people to achieve goals, but he thought we would not listen to him. When I asked him why, he said it was because he goes out and gets things done, either with his teammates or by himself. He did not think that we would agree with his methods, so there was no point in engaging with us.

He could not have been more wrong. At the next team meeting, I told him to lead the conversation. This guy came alive with motivational ideas, unique insights, and humor. I was blown away. Thank goodness I listened to his feedback.

Misunderstandings Can Be Avoided

You need to listen more. You must listen to your spouse, children, friends, and associates. Think about how many misunderstandings you could have avoided if you had just listened harder!

You want to be known as a thoughtful listener with incredible insight. That only occurs when you are a listener. Notice I did not say a "hearer." You may hear what people say, but are you listening for the meanings, thoughts, and agendas? Are you looking to gain wisdom or just taking a break from your turn to talk?

> *"Wisdom is principal; therefore, get wisdom.*
> *And with all your getting, get understanding."*
> Proverbs 4:7

Listening will produce wisdom, advice, and instruction that benefits you. When you listen, the future will not be a repetition of the past. Regardless of how good your history has been, you want it to improve. If your past has not been all you wanted it to be, then the future is still available to you. However, you will not gain the wisdom needed to affect your future if you do not listen more.

Providing an answer before you have all the information is a waste and foolishness, yet that is what many people do several times daily. Have you ever chomped at the bit to talk when someone else is still speaking? I have.

> *"A fool utters all his mind,*
> *but a wise man keeps it in until afterwards."*
> Proverbs 29:11

Every time I have been in that position, the point I wanted to make was lost since I was so focused on getting my turn to talk. When you are in that situation with such an attitude, you lose the opportunity to grow.

Allow Others To Shine

When you turn your ear toward someone else, you allow them to shine, but more importantly, you allow yourself to learn something you would not have otherwise known. There is something you can learn from everyone.

> *"Incline your ear and hear the words of the wise,*
> *and apply your heart to my knowledge."*
> *Proverbs 22:17*

Not paying attention to instruction is walking away from knowledge, which is the foundation of wisdom.

> *"Hear instructions, and be wise, and do not refuse it."*
> *Proverbs 8:33*

Without it, you have nothing to build upon to grow. Everything you need to develop is not already in your head. There is a great deal of information out in the world. You can attempt to read it all, but you also have people all around you every day who have experienced those exact moments. Learn from them.

Take pleasure in listening for understanding instead of expressing your opinion all the time. There is always plenty of time to express your opinion, but there are moments you will never experience or recover if you do not listen to others.

Plant The Seeds Of Listening

If this does not resonate with you, listen to others because you want them to hear what you say. Sow what you want to grow. Do you want people to listen to you? Then you need to plant the seeds of listening. The more you heed others, the more likely they will listen to you.

As a leader, you need to behave with a specific level of confidence so you can move forward without looking back doubtfully. It is essential to be engaged, reflective, and even sentimental. None of these emotional intelligence traits should hold you back when responding to your team thoughtfully. What will keep you back is isolating yourself from those you lead; not listening leads to isolation.

Do Not Isolate Yourself

It is not suitable for any leader to be alone. Great leaders surround themselves with close advisers or a circle of influence.

> *"Where there is no counsel, the people fall;*
> *but in the multitude of counselors there is safety."-*
> *Proverbs 11:14*

As much as being willing to surround yourself with like-minded individuals who challenge and encourage you is needed, if you fail to listen to them, then you will defeat the entire purpose.

It is not suitable for any leader to live in a vacuum. With your circle of influence, you have an excellent opportunity to discover where you are lacking in your listening skills. The same ideas that your teammates have communicated in the past will possibly be expressed by your circle of influence. Have you ever noticed how an idea sounds great when someone you consider an equal or a leader proposes it, but the same concept does not seem as brilliant if introduced by someone you do not respect?

Train Your Team To Exceed Your Abilities

If there was ever an essential lesson in "hiring up" and not down, it is that. Do not fear hiring someone superior in skill or coaching your team to exceed your abilities. The natural gifts and skills your team has within themselves are there to benefit not only them but you and the group as a whole.

As a leader, it is your job to encourage and promote those gifts. Supporting and advancing contributions can only occur when you listen to your team rather than just telling them what to do. You hired or inherited your team because you or someone else saw great potential in each of them. What if you did not see potential and, instead, hired a team with lesser abilities because you feared for your position? Now is the time to leave behind such fears and coach your team onward!

Nurture Your Teammates' Gifts

Cultivate your teammates' natural gifts and skills. However, you will only find out what those abilities are if you listen to them. Your role as their leader is thus to listen and bring positive change in their lives. Do not let a day go by without praising a team member and building them up to others. Always look to promote your teammates to a role of greater responsibility.

The reason to do all this is not to merely exhibit a lack of selfish ambition but to show your team in a meaningful way that you listen to them, care about them, and want to see them grow. Do not forget; your organization is not about achieving your personal goals. It is about attaining the organizational objectives, which include developing and expanding the capabilities of each member of your team.

Do not dismiss the feedback you receive without careful thought. This input could be the foundation for the next great idea that will energize you and your team. For that reason alone, you need to consider the feedback you receive from your teammates.

There is a time to remain steadfast in your decisions. That comes after thoughtful consideration and weighing of available options. To get to that point, you must seek and hear counsel from others. Their counsel, evaluated with purpose against the desired outcome, will propel you toward the results you want.

Do Not Fear Feedback

Do not fear hearing the feedback of others. So many people make this mistake, fearing to appear not having all the answers. Understand this: you do not have all the answers and should stop pretending you do. Continuing to behave self-deceptively based on what others will think when they discover you do not have all the answers is a waste of time and energy. Doing this only delays the success you desire.

The feedback you receive will not all be positive, but it needs to be heard and considered. Some of it will encourage you; some will make you think. Some feedback will make you laugh, and yet other types of critique will have the potential to offend. Remember, at all times, when you hear feedback, this is what the person thought at that moment would be best for you to understand. You learn a great deal and understand more about the people providing the input.

Three Lessons

The things people will say are all part of a learning experience. The first lesson is in how each person speaks. Are they serious, funny, sarcastic, cynical, or optimistic? Do they think about you and the opportunity to make a positive impact, or is this just the chance to get "something off their chest"?

The second lesson is in how well you respond. It is easy to ask for feedback, but going beyond simply hearing it to listen truly is not for the weak of heart. Have the personal courage to be able to process and withstand what some people will tell you. How many times has someone said something off-color or hurtful to you, but once called on, they replied that they were only joking? Here is the thing about jokes: they all have some basis in truth. You can let people get away with saying they were only joking, but do not delude yourself into thinking that is the case.

The third lesson is in what the words said mean to the person who spoke them and what they mean to you. Learning this lesson is a matter of processing what was said, sometimes admitting hard truths to yourself, and possessing a willingness to change. The change, though, only comes with time. You cannot change the past, but you can change the present, which will transform the future.

You must listen to your team and consider their feedback. If you fail to act on their input after thoughtful consideration, you are only deceiving yourself. Do not take the easy route of living in your fantasy. Be bold and make the changes needed based on the feedback of others.

Summary of Chapter 21

1. When you listen more, you will hear motivational ideas, unique insights, and humor that overcome misunderstandings.
2. Jumping to provide an answer will keep you from receiving all the information needed to provide a thorough answer.
3. To become a great leader, you will need to listen and receive the counsel of others.
4. Organizational goals will only be achieved with the team's collaboration and their ideas being heard, considered, and implemented where appropriate.
5. Asking for feedback is easy. Receiving it, considering it, and acting on it requires listening.

There is no wisdom nor understanding
nor counsel against the Lord.
Proverbs 21:30

Chapter 22:
Create a Safe Place

The rich and poor have this in common,
The Lord is the maker of them all.
Proverbs 22:2

Safe places are all the talk on college campuses. However, you need to create a different sort of safe place for you and your team.

Create A Safe Place For Ideas

I remember sitting in an executive meeting for the first time. Our CEO had invited me to join a group of executives from our company in a twice-monthly meeting. However, the conference did not include all the executives; three were excluded.

I was one of three invited from my level within the company and the only one from outside the home office region. This did not go over well with the three executives not invited, nor with my peers who were also not asked to attend. Frankly, I did not care. I was elated to be chosen to participate in what I was sure to be a great meeting of rousing discussions, seeking success for our organization and making it come to pass.

Was I ever wrong? The first meeting was painful in more ways than I will list, but primarily because some people were unwilling to provide feedback.

There were some in the meeting who were legitimately afraid to speak up. That was the day I learned that regardless of who you are or your level of success if you do not experience openness to your ideas, you will be afraid to share them.

Why People Fear Speaking Out

When you consider why people are unwilling to provide feedback, it is easy to assign fear as the primary one. Although anxiety is a motivator, there are several reasons people are unwilling to give feedback.

Your pride can create an atmosphere where others are unwilling to speak up. Do you act like you know all the answers? Do you always seem to know or at least think you know the correct action? Even when you compliment efforts made by a teammate, do you feel the need to tell them how you did it or how they could perform the action better? That is pride—stop it!

> *"Let nothing be done out of strife or conceit, but in humility let each esteem the other better than himself."*
> *Philippians 2:3*

Your judgmental demeanor can also create an atmosphere where others are unwilling to provide feedback. Do you always have to get in the last word? Have you made up your mind about what someone is going to say before they have completed their thought? When someone finishes speaking, do you think you could have presented in a superior way? That is being judgmental—stop it!

Your age, whether youthful or mature, can further create an uninviting atmosphere for critique. From one perspective, there is never *the* right age to be a leader. When you are young and have achieved promotions faster than your colleagues, they may still view you as the kid who knows nothing except the one idea that got you ahead. Your team may not share feedback with you because they think you are too young to understand. They may also think that you do not have enough sense to know a good idea from a bad one.

Sean Litvak

"Let no one despise your youth, but be an example to the believers in speech, in conduct, in love, in spirit, in faith, and in purity."
1 Timothy 4:12

As a mature leader with progressively higher demands, accountability, and complexity, your team may now look upon you as the doddering old fool who does not understand how the world has changed and why their new ideas are superior. They may also think that your past experiences keep you from having the sense to know a good idea from a bad one.

"Likewise, you younger ones, submit yourselves to the elders. Yes, all of you be submissive one to another and clothe yourselves with humility because God resists the proud but gives grace to the humble."
1 Peter 5:5

Do you see a pattern here? Understand that regardless of your age, it can be just one factor that will discourage others from speaking up.

Your argumentativeness will also create an unappealing environment for feedback. Strife is defined as "angry or bitter disagreement over fundamental issues; conflict." When you create a climate where it is you against another department, your team against another, or even worse, you against your team, the result will always be conflict. No one is comfortable presenting feedback in such situations.

"But if you have bitter envying and strife in your hearts, do not boast and do not lie against the truth. This wisdom descends not from above, but is earthly, unspiritual, and devilish. For where there is envying and strife, there is confusion and every evil work."
James 3:14-16

Why would your coworkers want to put their good ideas to the test of your confrontational, strife-loving, conflict-promoting self? Better to keep their thoughts to themselves and wait for the next leader who desires collaboration!

All of these situations and challenges have to do with you, and as such, you can change them quickly.

What you cannot change quickly, though, is when people experience fear, which stops them from sharing feedback. You may have heard that fear is nothing more than False Evidence Appearing Real (FEAR). It is the "real" part that slows people down and trips them up.

Do Not Take The Easy Path

Most people take the path of least resistance. That is why there are far more followers than leaders. Your job is to get your team to overcome their FEAR. It would help if you encouraged them to reach deep down and behave with the self-control and moderation they have learned throughout their lives. Giving in to FEAR is the easy road to failure now and in the future. Thus, personal accountability of self-control and moderation will assist you in defeating FEAR.

There is no FEAR of self-improvement. If you want your team to give feedback, then provide your organization with an opportunity for self-improvement. I was having lunch with members of my team years ago, and one of them was telling the other about a great webinar she had recently seen and how helpful they were. The other teammate asked her to send him the link to browse the webinars. I also asked her for the link. She then looked at me and told me I had sent her and the rest of my team the link a year ago, encouraging them to look through the options and work on self-improvement.

I had forgotten that I did so. However, look at the results: seed planted, the seed sown. This manager was okay when she started but had become exceptional over the last year. We always joked about how she had no issue like others in giving a critique when I asked for it. The webinars had destroyed the FEAR in her, and she was reaping the benefits.

Fear Is A Trap

FEAR is a snare waiting to trip you up. When you are constantly looking over your shoulder for what is coming next or executed more effectively, it keeps you from focusing on the moment and what you can do today. Please communicate with your team if they are hesitant to share good ideas. Make sure they understand that it will only be a matter of time before someone else comes up with the excellent idea they held back. The person willing to speak up will reap the rewards of collaboration, whereas the silent reaps nothing—what a waste of time and talent.

Do you want to hear other people's ideas? Then create a safe place for them to be understood. Encourage your team to speak up. Ask them to communicate even ideas they may feel are not worth hearing. Compliment good thoughts at every opportunity. Look for the quality in every statement (even in the wrong or ludicrous ideas), so you can complement it. I am not suggesting that you pander; however, you live in a cynically reinforced world. Almost everyone I know talks about how people look at things too negatively.

Be Transformational

Do not conform to the world, speaking and looking at things the way everyone else does. Instead, be transformational in how you interact with other people. Promote what is right, acceptable, and perfect in others. In whatever situation, create an encouraging safe place where others want to voice their ideas.

> *"Do not be conformed to this world, but be transformed by the renewing of your mind, that you may prove what is the good and acceptable and perfect will of God."*
> *Romans 12:2*

If you do this, you will be a catalyst for renewal, inspiring your colleagues to achieve greater discernment. In doing so, you will reap the benefits and revitalize your mind as well.

Build On Previous Ideas To Create Something New

Providing a safe place for ideas is crucial in order to build on previous notions, thus creating something not initially realizable and or even originally considered. Like other human achievements, the whole will be greater than the sum of its parts. Imagine all the ingredients of a cake; then imagine the cake itself. A cake does not look anything like the individual elements and is more than each of its components.

Original ideas may be excellent and worthwhile on their own. Still, when they are combined, they have the potential to be something extraordinary that encourages and affects everyone involved in the process. Another way to consider how creating a safe place will produce ideas that build on one another is by looking at how knives sharpen. Iron sharpens iron.

> *"Iron sharpens iron,*
> *so a man sharpens the countenance of his friend."*
> Proverbs 27:17

In this situation, it takes something similar to make an impact on a particular object.

The same is true for ideas. Without a safe haven for discussion, there will not be a constant flow of ideas, and you will thus become stunted in the ways of the past without a vision for the future.

Summary of Chapter 22

1. Provide a place where ideas are openly discussed; otherwise, individuals' anxiety and fear will keep them from speaking.
2. Overcoming your pride, judgmental demeanor, age, and argumentativeness will create an atmosphere where people are willing to speak and engage in conversation.
3. Those who desire self-improvement will not allow false evidence appearing real (FEAR) to get in the way.
4. As the leader or facilitator, look for every opportunity to compliment the individual's idea brought to the group.
5. The combination of common everyday ideas will have the potential to create something worthwhile and excellent, a greater sum than all of its parts.

Have I not written to you excellent things in counsels and knowledge, that I might make you know the certainty of the words of truth, that you might answer the words of truth to those who send to you?
Proverbs 22:20-21

Chapter 23:
Stares and Silence are Not Acceptable

Apply your heart to instruction, and your ears to the words of knowledge.
Proverbs 23:12

Questions responded to with blank stares and silence is not acceptable in a collaborative organization.

Silence Is Not Acceptable

Work hard; play hard. I remember that being the mantra we had at one of the companies I worked for. Looking back, I realized it was the company that I had worked for the most extended time. I can give you many reasons why I worked there for so long.

I liked the people; I was comfortable with them. I was able to grow in my role. I knew my voice was heard. Those are just a few of the reasons why I stayed there so long. This chapter, however, is not about any of those reasons.

It is about everything that I did not experience at that business. I cannot remember being in a meeting at this company and not having our questions answered, regardless of whether we were in a large or small group.

As a company, we were characterized by lively conversations, debates, and deep dives into details to determine root causes and more efficient strategies to provide our contracted services. Never do I recall sitting in a meeting where a question was met with a lack of response.

Ask Yourself Where You Failed

How often have you led a group through a conversation or learning process, and when you reached the point for interaction, you were greeted with silence? In such cases, what should be your response?

When this happens, you need to ask yourself where you failed. When you are the leader, ultimately, the lack of response is your fault. You have not driven the group to actively engage in discussion. You may have known those you are presenting to and understood the subject at hand, but without the proper application of the knowledge, true understanding has eluded you.

Build A Relationship With Those You Lead

You must build a relationship with those you are leading. The level of connection will vary if you are the frequent leader or an individual speaker brought in to train the group. Regardless, it is your responsibility to speak and behave in an accessible way.

There is great debate regarding if it is easier to draw in a group when they are familiar or unfamiliar with you. If they are familiar with you, then you have the advantage of historical relationships and common experiences. If they are unknown to you, then it is your responsibility to research the group in advance, find out everything you can, and apply this wisdom to create a connection.

Some will say that familiarity breeds contempt, while others will say the group will be cynical of anyone whom they do not know coming in to teach them about their own business. How you respond in such circumstances is always up to you. Never allow the situation to dictate the outcome. You can dictate the result by your preparedness, presentation, and confidence. People always smell fear.

Prepare More, Lead Less

You must spend a far more significant amount of time preparing than leading. Anticipating potential problems and challenges will pay off, while a lack of readiness will cause you great pain. Which would you rather do instead? Either you can put in the work in advance and succeed, or you will have to do the work later after you have already lost ground and, potentially, the respect of those you are leading.

The lack of response is never the fault of the group you are leading; it is your problem for not engaging them correctly. Whose fault is it when the horse does not drink? If you do not put water in front of the horse, it will not drink. The same is true when you are presenting to or leading a group.

When you first began reading this chapter, I am confident you thought it would be about confronting others for their lack of engagement. The real work starts when you realize the lack of commitment is not the fault of the team members but yours instead.

Commit To Being Different

You must commit to being different than those around you. It is too easy to be like everyone else. Of course, no one likes conflict. Unfortunately, nothing worthwhile has ever occurred without conflict of some kind and at some level.

You are reading this book now to improve yourself. You want to get ahead in some way. It may be at work, church, school, personal, or some other manner. The answer lies in what you are willing to do differently from the rest of the world.

Your willingness to move forward differently is not anything new. I do not pretend to have discovered this. It does, however, bear repeating. If you want something different, you must be willing to change into what you want to become. That transformational task is your challenge.

Be Honest With Yourself

You need to, daily, remind yourself of what you want to do. You need to, daily, examine the steps and actions you are taking and have a real conversation with yourself. Is what you are currently doing moving you along on the road to achieving your dreams, goals, and plans? Whether the answer is yes or no does not matter. What matters is that you have the personal courage and honesty to confront yourself about the outcome you are building.

You must test all your actions based on a willingness, to be honest with yourself. If you cannot be honest with yourself, then you will not be honest with anyone. Have the courage to judge yourself by your actions and not mere appearances. Only you can know if you are taking the steps needed to achieve your dreams.

Silence and blank stares within the context of a meeting are only symptoms of the problem. The real problem begins and ends with what you are willing or not willing to do to move forward personally and help others do the same. Confront yourself, not others.

The Measure Of Progress

How you measure progress is both an unwavering truth and, also, something relative, flexible, and adjustable over time. Let me explain.

The measure of progress is a truth that must remain constant if you want it to mean anything. Your ability to take honest measurements of your progress in multiple categories is paramount to recognizing when you are achieving, plateauing, backsliding, or learning. Consistently acknowledging the truth of your measurement is all-important.

You can lie to many people (colleagues, superiors, subordinates, relatives, friends, etc.), and they will not know the difference. However, you cannot lie to yourself. You will always know the truth, that is, where you stand in relation to your goals.

You must come to terms with this unwavering truth. To do anything less is self-sabotage.

Be Steadfast

To remain consistent in your measurement of progress, you must have a lifestyle of steadfastness. This means being immovable in personal honesty and always returning to the source and catalyst of what motivated you in the first place.

> *"My brothers, count it all joy when you fall into diverse temptations, knowing that the trying of your faith develops patience. But let patience perfect its work, that you may be perfect and complete, lacking nothing."*
> James 1:2-4

When you constantly remind yourself of the origin of your purposes, they will be easier to pursue.

The remainder of your foundational achievement desires will quell the fires of self-doubt and double-mindedness. Returning to the basics of your work as a measuring tool will ensure that your labor is not in vain. The only way your work will be in vain is if you walk away from it without completion. In such a case, you will always be wondering what could have been if you had completed what you set forth to do in the first place.

Be Flexible

Measuring your progress includes not giving in to the fears that are common to all of us. Instead, act with self-control, which is something everyone desires to achieve. This deliberate self-control will reward you with not just knowledge of your progress but also the wisdom of how you moved forward and what to do next. Now, this is where flexibility comes into play.

As you move back and forth between achieving, plateauing, backsliding, and learning, you will eventually know when a door has opened to another room. What I mean is that, as you progress, you will ultimately see when you have genuinely done so. It is then that the measurement of progress becomes relative, flexible, and adjustable.

Learning Is A Process

Think back throughout your life. Do you measure your progress today in the same way that you did years ago? If so, you have not challenged yourself enough to have moved forward. That is a different issue. The way you measure progress must be rooted in the unwavering truth of measurement; however, the analysis adjusts over time. The challenge is that you are not always aware of this adjustment until you have moved beyond where you were long ago.

However, "long ago" does not necessarily relate to time as it does to achievement and expectation. Think of yourself as a student. The lessons you learned in preschool, elementary, middle, and high school are all very different. The same is true of the lessons learned in college as an undergraduate, graduate, or doctoral student. Consistency in the measurement of progress occurs in a very similar way. Flexibility is what you are measuring. The personal discipleship of your life is an accumulative process; it is a mountain that you climb.

What you need to understand ultimately is that the foundational tactics are the same even when the end goal has shifted.

Summary of Chapter 23

1. The silence of your team is not their inability to speak – it is your failure to draw them out.
2. The time you spend preparing for interaction with your team is in direct correlation to their active engagement.
3. Your courage and honesty to personally change will draw out your coworkers.
4. The measurements of your consistency and steadfastness are lifestyle choices that cannot be hidden behind deception.
5. The same discipline you used to learn is what you need to lead your team out of silence.

*The father of the righteous will greatly rejoice,
and he who fathers a wise child will have joy of him.
Proverbs 23:24*

Chapter 24:
Leading in a Vacuum Never Produces Results

A wise man is strong; yes, a man of knowledge increases strength. For by wise counsel, you will wage your war, and in multitude of counselors there is safety.
Proverbs 24:5-6

Coaching and leading in a vacuum
never produce the results you desire.

Do Not Lead In A Vacuum

I had an interesting experience that has stuck with me to this day. At one time, I led a team of introverts. Every single person that reported directly to me was my social opposite. It was one of the most exceptional experiences of my life.

We had what each other required. Each of them needed a push or an encouragement to risk doing what did not come naturally. They were all great managers but appeared to be slow in considering options and even slower to put them in play. In most cases, their direct reports had come to me, asking that I get most of them to make a decision, either positive or negative.

I had the exact opposite issue. I would make decisions quickly, think out loud, and try anything when issues were recurring. I needed to be more like them.

Complement Each Other

We complemented each other. I challenged them to be more like me and take chances. At the same time, I told them that I would become more like them in my responses: thoughtful, empathetic, and moderate.

What a team we made!

Listening to feedback provides you with greater insight, awareness, and discernment. As I stated earlier, you must listen to others' critiques, especially when you ask for them in the first place.

Think of the feedback as advice. With all the information at hand, you now have the opportunity to filter it and decide what is worthwhile and what is not. Do not think that because specific feedback makes you uncomfortable, it is not worth considering. Sometimes, the critique that creates the most awkward feelings within you is that which contains the best advice. If you can get over your fear and listen to the information, then you will gain the wisdom needed for today and the future.

Growth Leads To Wisdom

However, if you give in to fear, and choose not to listen to the advice and instruction from others, then you will rightly be labeled a fool. Being wise in your own eyes does create a feeling of justification, but ultimately life is not about how you feel, but, instead, what you are willing to push your way through to grow.

> *"Woe to those who are wise in their own eyes,*
> *And prudent in their own sight!"*
> *Isaiah 5:21*

Growth will make you wise, and the more wisdom you gain, the more advice you will be prone to consider.

As understanding builds block upon block, you will discover that you know less than you first thought. Simultaneously, you will realize that you must listen a great deal to the advice of others to achieve the desired outcomes.

Some people will provide feedback that has no other purpose than to frustrate and exasperate you. They do not have your continued growth as part of their plan, far from it. Instead, they would rather lead you in circles until you are willing to give in and follow them out of sheer desperation for inner peace. It is thus imperative that you recognize these individuals immediately for who they are.

Have Faith In Yourself

Also, consider that your unwillingness to listen to the advice of others puts your weakness and lack of personal confidence on display for everyone to see. No one wants to work with those who lack confidence.

Furthermore, your lack of faith will drive away those who can and want to help you in life. Your opinion will become worthless to them because if you cannot believe in yourself, then why should others think you have anything worthwhile to say?

Instead, you should measure the feedback from the perspective of the glass being half full as opposed to half empty. Even those people with whom you have little in common or agree can have something worthwhile to say. So, listen to their critiques, embrace them, and make them positive in every area of your life!

Coach For Excellence

The feedback you receive will also dictate how you focus on coaching your team. Coaching in a business situation is not dissimilar from the sports context. The differences are between the coach and the student.

Your coaching needs to focus on the individual's strengths more so than their weaknesses. Evaluate the individual you are coaching to determine where their strengths and weaknesses are across the spectrum of needed skills. You are likely more gifted in certain areas than others. The last person you want on your team is the generalist or utility player. Some see that as versatility when it is, in fact, an expression of mediocrity.

Concentrate instead on the subject matter that your colleagues are good at, with the intent to make them great. Coach them to exceed your skill set in each area that is their greatest strength.

> *"but those who wait upon the Lord shall renew their strength; they shall mount up with wings as eagles, they shall run and not be weary, and they shall walk and not faint."*
> Isaiah 40:32

The person who has the foundational skills of excellence in a particular subject is more likely to improve in that area than where remedial skill-building is required. Therefore, assist your team in becoming subject matter experts.

How To Coach

You may ask, how is it possible to coach someone to exceed your mastered skillset? Think about the coach of any team. Is the coach the best at any position on the team? No. What the coach has is the knowledge of *how* to be the best in every situation.

The coach's job is to teach each player to make them the best at what they already exceed in. The coach's ability to transfer knowledge and bring out the best in each player is their true talent. The same is right for you in any leadership role.

Coaching in this way may appear counterintuitive to many. Coaches have traditionally focused on improving weaknesses. While that is beneficial, the higher focus of a coach should be to improve the existing skills to an outstanding level.

Everyone Benefits

Who would benefit from your efforts? Many think the answer to this question is based on your motivation, but the solution is far simpler than that. Everyone involved will benefit if your motives are not self-centered.

Think about it. When coached, the benefit is obvious. The coach is working to improve your skillset, situation, and outcome. It is thus easy to see how you advance. As you learn new skills and how to handle situations, you experience growth that will propel you further along in your dreams.

Summary of Chapter 24

1. Look at the differences between team members and yourself as complementary strengths to be leveraged for mutual benefit.
2. Fear of the feedback that makes you uncomfortable is how fools respond. Push through the awkward feelings to achieve growth.
3. Coach teammates to improve their strengths, especially when they have the capacity to exceed your abilities.
4. Everyone benefits when the leader recognizes coaching as a two-way road and the motives are not self-centered.

If you faint in the day of adversity, your strength is small.
Proverbs 24:10

Chapter 25:
Do Not Become Frustrated

A word fitly spoken is like apples of gold in settings of silver.
Proverbs 25:11

If everyone listened to what you said and agreed with you without questions, then you would be a dictator, not a leader.

Avoid Frustration

I used to do something that frustrated my children to no end. I did it in jest (sort of), but it became a habit that only as they got older did I find out it bothered them.

I gave them instructions, raised my hands to the right of my head, clapping them together twice, and then said, "So let it be written, so let it be done." This was my way of being humorous and direct at the same time about the tasks I wanted them to do.

They never laughed—ever.

It was not until they got into their twenties that they told me how they hated it and found it demeaning. I was surprised. I thought it was funny and got my point across.

My kids told me that they felt as though they had to follow what I told them when I ended the direction with the clap and that phrase. That's all they understood.

Now that they are older, there is no need to clap and use such phrases any longer. Now, however, they were pushing back against how I made the point. Therefore, we talked about the whole matter, and I explained my reasons.

In a business context, as in family matters, you must discuss any issues that you are avoiding. Do all that is needed to communicate to others that you have gained an understanding.

Prepare For Criticism

Regardless of how many times you have gone through what I am about to describe, it is always surprising and painful. Tell me if this has happened to you.

You have been newly promoted to a leadership position, whether at work, a professional association, a faith-based organization, or a club. You are excited about being recognized by your peers for your achievements and are equally enthusiastic about the recognition that has earned you this position. You have received encouragement and praise from your colleagues. Now, you have the real opportunity to make a difference.

Then it happens. The first move you make to implement or even discuss a change that you know will have an impact, and, *bam!* You receive pushback from all those colleagues that were so supportive. Were you prepared for this? Most likely, the answer is a resounding no.

The only person you have to blame for this lack of preparation in such challenging situations is yourself. In a leadership position, we are all called upon to be ready in every season for every situation. Being prepared does not mean that you have all the answers at hand. It means not being caught off guard when called upon to find the answers.

"Preach the word, be ready in season and out of season,
reprove, rebuke, and exhort, with all patience and teaching.
For the time will come when people will not endure sound doctrine, but they will
gather to themselves teachers in accordance with their own desires, having itching

ears, and they will turn their ears away from the truth and turn to myths."
2 Timothy 4:2-4

How do you do that?

Learn How To Critique Others

Do not praise others without good reason. The best thing you can do to encourage your colleagues other than to praise them is to examine their ideas and gently correct their potential failings. The challenge is not in actually inspecting possible faults. Rather, the problem is in how you do that and how you communicate it with your colleagues.

Such communication of corrective actions must be interlaced with encouragement, which is based on patience and teaching. If you only seek out the faults with someone's idea or plan, then you will be labeled a narcissist with a bad attitude. Conversely, if all you do is praise individuals for their ideas, regardless of if they are valid, insightful, or will work, then you are creating narcissists who will not see their faults and will be unable to think critically.

The balance of praise and corrective conversations must occur in advance of any promotion you receive if you expect people to respect your leadership once promoted. Your challenge is to behave like a leader before you become one. Live your life congratulating others profusely while simultaneously correcting their mistakes respectfully.

Becoming that person before being promoted will put you far ahead of others who have not developed in such a manner. Change happens, but one thing that does not change is that people will always want to work with someone who is insightful, self-aware, and humble. Prepare yourself and become that person now so you can easily make the transition to leadership later.

You are capable of handling anything, even the pushback you receive from other people.

Proverbs for Leadership

Practice Self-Control

When you experience opposition, realize that it is something you can handle and is not beyond your capabilities.

"I know both how to face humble circumstances and how to have abundance. Everywhere and in all things, I have learned the secret, both to be full and to be hungry, both to abound and to suffer need. I can do all things because of Christ who strengthens me."
Philippians 4:12-13

You have the strength to maintain a sound mind and control your response. Never give in to the temptation to give someone a piece of your mind. Nothing good ever comes from losing control or simply telling someone everything you are thinking. Some thoughts are best kept to yourself.

Freely voicing what you are thinking may lead to an even higher fever pitch than you thought possible. As you become angrier, the issue is no longer about with whom you are speaking. It becomes about voicing even more outrage. The battle stops being with that person and becomes a fight between you and your repressed frustrations.

"And observe ships. Though they are so great and are driven by fierce winds, yet they are directed with a very small rudder wherever the captain pleases.
Even so, the tongue is a little part of the body and boasts great things. See how great a forest a little fire kindles. The tongue is a fire, a world of evil. The tongue is among the parts of the body, defiling the whole body, and setting the course of nature on fire, and it is set on fire by hell. All kinds of beasts, and birds, and serpents, and things in the sea are tamed or have been tamed by mankind. But no man can tame the tongue. It is an unruly evil, full of deadly poison.
With it we bless the Lord and Father, and with it we curse men, who are made in the image of God. Out of the same mouth proceed blessing and cursing. My brothers, these things ought not to be so. Does a spring yield at the same opening sweet and bitter water? Can the fig tree, my brothers, bear olives, or a vine, figs? So, no spring can yield both salt water and fresh water."
James 3:4-12

Do not make that mistake. Words spoken cannot be taken back, even when you apologize. Whatever you say in a state of rage will never be forgotten. Giving in to anger is not what you should do. You want to overcome challenges, not create new ones.

Substitute Physical Exercise For Battle

That said, you need to blow off steam from time to time. The path of least resistance is to simply blow it off on someone else. Instead, go work out and do something physical (and I am not talking about punching a wall).

You can fight, but in the modern day, the battle has become one of words and mind. For many of you, the physical struggle is not part of your daily life, and because of that, you have become weak and soft. In addition, due to a lack of physical exertion, you have lost the outlet for exercising aggression from yourselves. You cannot carry such high levels of mental and emotional stress. You must release those stresses through physical activity.

Run, lift weights, do aerobics, plank, swim, whatever; do something that stresses you physically and, at the same time, releases the stresses within your mind and emotions. The substitution of physical exercise for physical battle will prevent you from fighting with words when situations and people become challenging. The temptation to push back against those that struggle against you will not lead to success and prosperity. It will drive you further away from it.

Your Greatest Challenge

Do not take the challenges, criticisms, and battles personally that you will face during your career. I have heard it said that different genders, races, nationalities, or religions have it more difficult than others. That is foolishness. The greatest challenge you face is the battle within your head by taking the words and criticisms of others personally.

Proverbs for Leadership

*"Therefore, my beloved brothers, let every man be swift to hear,
slow to speak, and slow to anger,
for the anger of man does not work the righteousness of God."
James 1:19-20*

It does not matter who or what you are. There will be those who do not like you and will do whatever is possible to promote themselves. Some will even go a step further not just to help themselves but degrade the respect others have for you. The higher you rise, the more you are considered a threat by others. Most people do not like those who succeed. You live in a jealous society where individuals can decide that the hard work you have done is not what produced your results. They believe that you have some level of entitlement; you have cheated to prosper, or, even worse, you were just lucky.

The only entitlement or luck you experience builds on the foundation of hard work, a sound mind, and treating others with respect. If you do not achieve all three, you will fail, becoming bitter like those who insult anyone who does manage to succeed.

People are bound to their efforts. Those who throw up energy like mud against a wall waiting to see what sticks will view you negatively. Do not let this bother you; it is not worth your time. You cannot change the minds of those who do not want to look beyond their self-pity any more than you can change the direction of the wind. You may be able to harness the wind, but you will not alter its course.

Build A Culture Of Collaboration

The level of effort you put forth is essential. Equally important is the credit you give the members of your team. Your personal success is not what should be driving you. Instead, think about the success of your organization. If the team wins, you all win. If you win, the team may still fail, but as leader of the group, you will be responsible.

Looking back at your career, remember when you were happiest. I know the immediate thoughts may be personal victories, but I am convinced that once you give the question considerable thought, you will find the happiest moments have been when you achieved success with your team. The thrill of successful collaboration overrules any personal victory.

Stop taking the barbs of those who disdain your victory personally. Instead, focus on building a team that has a vested interest in collaborative and shared triumph. Forming a cooperative team produces a "when you win, we all win" culture, and then you will have others to celebrate with!

Summary of Chapter 25

1. Your tone and mannerism can frustrate others.
2. Be prepared in every situation to the best of your wisdom, understanding, and knowledge.
3. Challenges, obstacles, and pushback will happen; your soul, spirit, and body can handle them.
4. Words spoken thoughtlessly and in haste injure and can never be taken back.
5. Get into a physical activity regimen to work out your own frustrations.
6. Take an inventory of your happiest moments, and you will find they were when your team succeeded, not your own personal victories.

By long forbearing is a prince persuaded,
and a soft tongue breaks the bone.
Proverbs 25:15

Chapter 26: Shared Growth

As a dog returns to its vomit, so a fool returns to his folly.
Proverbs 26:11

The teammates that respectfully challenge your point of view and ideas are the best people to associate with for shared growth.

What Shared Growth Means

Remember the company that I wrote about earlier in Chapter 23? The one where we worked hard and played hard? This story is about them.

We would often have meetings to review the previous quarter and plan for the next one. (Back then, everyone had to travel to the city that housed corporate headquarters.) Yes, we had our own internal quarterly business reviews.

During these meetings, each of the leaders would make presentations all day long about what was happening in their geographic sector: the good, the bad, and the confusing. As a team, we would solve each other's issues.

We were very driven individuals who were not shy about voicing our thoughts. We were all nice about what we said, except for one guy, but that is another story. However, you might not have thought we were being helpful if you were listening to us. We had a philosophy that could be summed up this way: if you have thin skin, then you won't make it here.

It was true. We were biting one another in the funniest of ways at times and behaved even somewhat disrespectfully. The way we spoke to one another would not work in most businesses today. Do you know why it worked?

Because we trusted each other, do not get me wrong. We each wanted to have the best run and the most profitable region, but we also wanted the company to excel. That is what brought us together and allowed the banter to be bearable, even when it was borderline rude. It was about trust and shared goals.

Silence Is Not Golden

You may believe silence is golden, but I do not subscribe to that position. I like to talk, and I like the sound of people talking. Yes, I love banter. Nothing has the potential to bring forth great ideas than individuals talking up a storm about a topic.

Listening to the talk of many can cleanse away old thoughts and ideas and wipe the slate clean. When you are talking with those in your circle of influence, you have the best opportunity to gain the knowledge of many, which leads to wisdom.

It is crucial that you thoughtfully choose with whom you banter. Your speech, and the speech you expose yourself to, should always be gracious and seasoned with thoughtfulness. This will result in a positive exchange of ideas. If you just banter with anyone, there is a much higher potential for strife, contradiction, and arguments.

Test those with whom you speak regularly. Do the people you joke with have a positive outlook, or do they see clouds on a clear day? Are they people who are optimistic but prepared for the worst, or do they always look at every situation as a potential worst-case scenario? The time you spend talking with people will reveal the truth about them.

Talk at length with those who you are considering inviting into your group, individually first, if possible. I am not suggesting interviewing them—just talking. People have a way of eventually defaulting back to their worldview. The negative person, for example, will always attempt to block the light of optimism. They may not be successful, but why even allow them the opportunity?

The Bible tells you the tongue is like the rudder of a ship.

> *"And observe ships. Though they are so great and are driven by fierce winds, yet they are directed with a very small rudder wherever the captain pleases. 5 Even so, the tongue is a little part of the body and boasts great things. See how great a forest a little fire kindles."*
> James 3: 4 - 5

Imagine that. The rudder of the boat directs where the ship heads. The same is true with an individual's tongue in conversation. You want to only allow people into your brainstorming session who desire the same shared outcome of the group. At all costs, do your best to remove those that have personal agendas or enjoy managing chaos.

Such individuals will lead you astray with their foolishness. To allow them in and follow them is being disobedient to yourself. The creators of chaos find pleasure in running you through a circular maze of conversation and actions. They are full of malice, envy, and hatred and, ultimately, are some of the most insecure people you will meet.

Instead, maintain the peace and avoid chaos. Listen to what others have to say before you let them in your circle of influence, let alone influence you. When you hear them speak, listen to what they are saying, including the meaning behind it, the motivation, and the agendas. Is their advice designed to help the group, or just place them in a position of power so they can swoop in and save the day?

Carefully consider what others say, including their banter. If you do so, both you and the group will experience growth.

Just like you may at times have the proclivity to think that you are always right, your teammates have that ability also. Some would call this arrogance. I have no problem with someone who has that level of confidence. Frankly, I would prefer to work with someone who thought their ideas were correct instead of a person who believed their ideas and thoughts were always wrong.

It is similar to working with someone who always has a negative view or statement to make. Give me the optimistic arrogant person who thinks they have all the answers. If you listen to them long enough, they may have more answers than you realize. In any case, they will have more answers than the person who thinks they are never right.

Find The Nuggets Of Truth

Separate the wheat from the chaff.

> *"His fan is in His hand, and He will thoroughly clean His floor and gather His wheat into the granary, but He will burn up the chaff with unquenchable fire."*
> Matthew 3:12

Find the nuggets of truth that are helpful versus the chunks that are nothing more than an empty shell. You need to determine what are the excellent gifts of people that do not have a personal agenda or shadow within them.

Listening to and bantering with such individuals allow you to participate in a quest for knowledge that will, hopefully, lead to further wisdom. The challenge is not getting tricked into a situation, believing something that is not true or comes with someone's personal agenda.

When listening to the ideas of others, however, do not swerve from your core beliefs. Your fundamental expectations are anchored in truth and are not subject to the whims of the world and what is right and what is wrong at the moment.

You should consider slowly and patiently the changes to be made based on the statements of others. Snap decisions will break you down the road.

Anything that is worth implementing requires a thoughtful process. Do not dread potential changes, but do not avoid them either.

Ideas And Prosperity

As beauty is in the eye of the beholder, the same can be said for a good idea. So often, what is considered a better idea than another is a matter of perspective. It would be best to remember that the plan you think is terrific and will solve whatever problem the team is facing is just one of many ideas on a continuum that will provide the desired results. Still, which is better or best?

A better idea is one that creates prosperity. Prosperity, in the lowest sense, is monetary, but there is so much more to understand when defining what success is or, in the case of an idea, profitable. (The Seven Laws of Prosperity, May 2, 2019 – https://blog.kcm.org/the-7-laws-of-prosperity/) A profitable idea will not only solve the problem at hand but also teach something to those participating in the solution. Better ideas teach long-lasting lessons.

Better ideas are also those that correct individuals. Think about it. How often have you heard an idea that was either a rehash of something that did not work in the past or would make a bad situation worse? A better approach is one that allows the individual to correct their way of thinking without causing them to lose the respect of the team or respect for themselves.

Competence

A better idea is also one that trains your team. Everyone should desire to grow, and that means continual training. The best teammates and those in leadership want to participate in training and, frankly, have it be a part of their everyday life. The better ideas train people to think in a new and different way, overcoming obstacles of the past and moving on to the future.

Better ideas make you competent. What is competency? "Having the necessary ability, knowledge, or skill to do something successfully." Present better approaches to the group from which everyone will learn. Everyone is skilled at performing different tasks at a higher level. With training, you become equipped with the skills and knowledge necessary to work through challenges effectively and efficiently.

Humility

Being open to better ideas will enable others to shine before the team. It also allows you to demonstrate to the team that the creation of ideas is not just up to the leader but is something in which everyone can participate. Being humble and embracing others' ideas, especially those that are better than your own, is a lesson you need to learn and repeat often.

Behaving with such humility communicates that you know you cannot do everything on your own, and all great ideas do not only come from you but also. Your consistency in this approach lets others know that you believe everyone has something to learn from someone else.

> *"Let nothing be done out of strife or conceit, but in humility let each esteem the other better than himself."*
> Philippians 2:3

The way you communicate knowledge to others will allow them to relax and listen for those ideas that make them better people while at the same time encouraging the team.

Summary of Chapter 26

1. If you have thin skin, you will not grow or handle associating with those who are growing
2. Only banter and brainstorm with those who desire the same shared outcome of the group.
3. Avoid those who create chaos for the sake of chaos. They are full of malice, envy, and hatred and, ultimately, are some of the most insecure people you will meet.
4. Be open-minded, but do not allow persuasion to sway you from your foundational beliefs that are built on truth.
5. Profitable ideas solve problems.
6. Your consistent walking in humility lets others know that you believe everyone has something to learn from someone else.

A lying tongue hates those who are afflicted by it,
and a flattering mouth works ruin.
Proverbs 26:28

Chapter 27:
How to Help Others Find Their Joy

*Do not boast about tomorrow, for you do not know
what a day may bring forth.
Proverbs 27:1*

Allow everyone the opportunity to find their joy, but do not let unhappy people drag you down in the process.

Some People Are Never Happy

We have all had that boss: the person that, regardless of what you did or achieved, was never satisfied. Sometimes that boss could be jealous of what you have achieved or insecure for some other reason. What this person failed to realize is that your success was also their success as part of their team. Your success and lack of greater supervision freed them to achieve new greatness with other members of the organization or on a personal project.

Sadly, that does not always happen. The reason is that some people are never happy. They have lost their joy and view every situation as a worst-case scenario. When the sun is shining, they point out the only cloud. When you find a saving that positively affects the bottom line and improves productivity, they chastise you for not first receiving approval.

Working With An Unhappy Boss

In the early days of the internet, our company had a dial-up service. For those who do not know what I mean, back then, we accessed the internet by dialing a landline phone and laying the receiver in a unique cradle while loud shrill noises connected your computer to the World Wide Web. Eventually, the computer had a modem built-in and was plugged directly into an electrical outlet. However, only one computer at a time could connect to the internet.

When high-speed service first rolled out, phone companies were anxious to sell it. These were the first bundled packages. I changed the phone service to our office. I canceled the line we used for internet connections, ordered high-speed service, and lowered our monthly invoice. I did not ask for permission. Why would I? This improved our service at a lower rate. There was no reason to request permission.

That was not what my boss thought. He claimed to be upset because I had made a significant decision without approval—at least, that is what I was told. What angered my boss was that I had better service and a lower rate than his office. Also, he was chronically in a bad mood.

Learning to work with a constantly miserable supervisor is excellent training for coaching an unhappy teammate. It is not the most enjoyable practice, but great training nonetheless!

Prepare For The Inevitable

There are certain situations and people that you will always come into contact with during your life. These situations and people are as inevitable as death and taxes. You should thus embrace the inevitability and prepare yourself for them.

Some people pull life out of the air in a room and are consistently negative regardless of the situation. That same person is only happy when there is chaos, which they are glad to fix with a grin, and then tell everyone, "See, I told you so."

There is little use in getting angry or upset with these people. They are in your life like the sun that rises and sets each day. You will know them, but they should never be a part of your circle of influence unless you are looking for someone to drag down your positive outlook.

> *"My brothers, count it all joy when you fall into diverse temptations, knowing that the trying of your faith develops patience. But let patience perfect its work, that you may be perfect and complete, lacking nothing."*
> James 1:2-4

Potentially, you have no choice but to work with such characters. Sometimes they are assigned to you in one sense or another. For example, you may have inherited them as part of your team. Or, you move to another company with a new supervisor and different contacts. Partnering with these individuals when you have positive expectations comes with a price.

Learn From Negative People

The price you have to pay is finding more time to spend with your circle of influence and developing further personal growth techniques in order not to succumb to the constant bombardment of negativity. These individuals will define themselves as "realists"; however, if that is a reality, then fantasy should look better to you.

I am not saying that there is nothing to learn from negative situations. Indeed, you initially learn how not to live your life. However, to be always cynical takes far more energy than living life with a positive outlook. If you want more power in your life, then avoid chronic negativity.

Still, without negative people, there would not be any problems to fix.

> *"Do not be deceived: "Bad company corrupts good morals."*
> *1 Corinthians 15:33*

Think about the teams with whom you work. Is it not the negative person consistently bemoaning challenges, complaining without offering solutions, or taking the road of victimization, saying they know how to fix the situation but do not have the authority to make the necessary changes?

Some of the best fixes I ever implemented were those where I did not have the authority to make the decision. It is a risk, but what is life if not full of dangers? The commoner never takes risks and just sits back and lets life pass them by.

You can live that life, but if you do, you will never be fulfilled and will not achieve what you were created to accomplish.

Understanding Pessimistic People

Now that you know there are consistently negative people prowling the earth, waiting to put a kibosh on your ideas and a damper on your life in general, what are you going to do to understand them so you can work with them productively?

You can attempt to correct and train them to have a different outlook. However, what is the purpose of doing that, and how will they view such an interaction? These negative individuals are historically acting out on their insecurities. How do I know that? Sometimes, when I feel insecure in certain situations, negativity clouds my mind and thoughts.

If someone is behaving negatively because of their insecurity, the last thing they want to hear is a different point of view. I am not suggesting that you join such a pity party. Your efforts will be better spent searching for solutions to the challenge at hand and not immediately sharing them with the unhappy people in your life. They have already decided on the route that is best for them. It will bring everyone else nothing but challenges, pain, and frustration.

Do not give in to the pain, suffering, and frustration brought about by the pessimistic people in your life. Although you would like to break them out of their negativity, the one thing that will bring them some perverse level of joy is seeing you get dragged down with them.

Encourage Accomplishing Of Goals

Instead, appeal to their sense of accomplishment for the task at hand. Even people who are unhappy are not without the desire to fulfill the required project; the group, however, has to complete it. The best thing you can do is stay your usual optimistic self regardless of any verbal barbs thrown at you. Keep moving forward in a positive way to complete the task while removing obstacles from their path. You may not receive credit, but is your life about receiving credit, or is it about doing a job well done for its own sake?

Understanding the morose people in your life, their motivations, and how to work with them is a skill in high demand. Anyone can work with positive people who desire to move forward as a team. It is the rare individual that can do that with the negative, unhappy person while maintaining the right attitude.

> *"Therefore, since we have been justified by faith,*
> *we have peace with God through our Lord Jesus Christ, through whom we also have access by faith into this grace in which we stand, and so we rejoice in hope of the glory of God.*
> *Not only so, but we also boast in tribulation, knowing that tribulation produces patience, patience produces character, and character produces hope."*
> *Romans 5:1-4*

Your understanding of such people will save you from the contradictions that are easy to experience. Working with them will be like anything else that you set to accomplish in life. Have a dream but develop a good working relationship with others. Set a goal but be honest when in conversation with a gloomy person. Make a plan but determine in advance how much interaction is necessary with a challenging person in order to reach your goal. Be willing to adjust as you receive feedback, regardless of whether it is negative or positive.

Prepare With A Positive Outlook

Now that you know how to deal with an unhappy co-worker, how are you going to prepare yourself for the time spent with them?

Be ready always for their verbal barbs.

> *"But sanctify the Lord God in your hearts.*
> *Always be ready to give an answer to every man who asks you for a reason for the hope that is in you, with gentleness and fear. Have a good conscience so that evildoers who speak evil of you and falsely accuse your good conduct in Christ may be ashamed."*
> *1 Peter 3:15-16*

Their attempts to correct in order to bring you down will be forthcoming from all directions. Do you know who likes positive people with a vision? Other positive people. Do you know who does not like positive people with a vision? Everyone else.

As you are working out your vision, understand that challenges will come, including sometimes from those who were once your greatest cheerleaders and encouragers. Many people are happy that you have a dream and a vision; however, once you start succeeding at what you are doing, the criticisms will begin.

Do not let this be a surprise. Look around the world; do you want to be like almost everyone you see, or do you prefer to be in an elite, select group of people who move forward toward their dreams and goals? You cannot be friends with everyone and achieve what you desire. Something has got to give.

Be Ready For Radical Changes

Be prepared that there will come a time when you need to make radical changes in your life. Those changes will begin internally at first: how you think, what you read, and how you spend your time. You will likely be invited to join in on conversations to discuss how wrong everything is, but that does not mean you have to participate. Have some backbone and choose to either leave the room or just be quiet. Silence speaks volumes, as does absence from useless meetings meant only to stir people up.

You can encourage others to move forward, but ultimately it is their decision. You cannot remove people from your family or your company simply because they do not agree with you. You can, however, choose not to join them in their critical thinking and bad attitudes. Eventually, the choices you make will not even require you to make such decisions. As you thrive and progress on your path, those who are always unhappy will cut you out of their lives. I have seen it happen time and again.

Coach People Up Or Out

You can move forward with positive expectations, happiness, and a plan, and those who would rather wallow in their insecurity will eventually leave you alone. I have heard it said that you need to coach people up or out. One way of doing this is by example. You are an example of how to move forward in life, both professionally and personally.

Those who can take it will join you, and those who cannot leave. Once the negative people go, you will have much more time on your hands because you will discover that what they were doing was working against the team's efforts. People who are coached out will help the team to achieve more.

However, never push them out. Instead, help despairing people with everything you have. Remember, though, even you cannot force them to drink water on a hot day.

Summary of Chapter 27

1. Your success affects others and allows them to be loosed to achieve new greatness.
2. Although you will work with individuals who attempt to drag you down, there is little use in getting angry or upset with these people.
3. Without negative people, there would not be problems to fix. Take the risk and fix their problems.
4. Embracing the lifestyle of understanding the unhappy, negative people in your life, what motivates them, and how to work with them is a skill in high demand.
5. Be ready always for the verbal barbs you will receive.
6. You can encourage others to move forward, but ultimately it is their decision.

As the refining pot for silver, and the furnace for gold,
so is a man to his praise.
Proverbs 27:21

Chapter 28:
Walking in Authority and
the Responsibility that Comes with It.

The wicked flee when no man pursues,
but the righteous are bold as a lion.
Proverbs 28:1

You have great authority as a leader,
and with that power comes even greater responsibility.

Beware Of Corporate Traps

Several years ago, I had a conversation with our one-time human resources leader at a company where I was once employed. It occurred during our senior leadership team meeting, but it turned into a talk between our human resources and myself.

The HR leader was advocating a corporate style of terminating the bottom 10 percent of performers within our management team every year. This plan was supposed to occur regardless of whether the individual achieved their targets and goals for the year.

I had a problem with this for several reasons. The goals that we had set as a leadership team were consistently published 30 days past the start of the year. The areas where a manager would be measured changed based on the fluctuating focus of our leadership team. There was also a lack of transparency around the data used to measure achieving the goals.

The main reason I was against this method is that we did not have a process in place to allow individuals to improve. Also, all individuals at a specific level of management were not held to the same criteria. Here we were expecting our team to coach other teams to grow, yet we were failing by not giving them the tools needed.

We had fallen into a trap: culling management instead of improving individuals. Thankfully, this plan did not happen because the Human Resources leader failed to produce the documents necessary to measure success. Looking back on it, I see the irony.

When you have the opportunity to coach a team, it is a gift you should not take lightly. I have seen leaders of various skills in many settings. Whether it be in little league baseball or on the business front, the lessons you can learn are the same. The coach that embraces their role with confident humility will be the most successful.

Coach To An Individual's Strength

I have adopted a coaching strategy that is also a way of life:

> *"Finally, my brothers, be strong in the Lord*
> *and in the power of His might."*
> *Ephesians 6:10.*

You need to coach an individual's strengths, as well as improve weaknesses. The latter is also required, but if you only focus on weaknesses, the person being trained will likely grow frustrated.

As a leader, coaching someone's strengths will bring about a much more positive interaction. The potential to become frustrated is far less when you are seeking to achieve incremental improvement in an area that is already a strength versus one that begins a weakness. However, I suggest alternating between strength coaching and weakness coaching.

You must keep an even demeanor about you. When you are only coaching in order to see a significant improvement, you may become discouraged by what appears to be a lack of progress. Use the cookie approach to giving feedback. Begin with praise, move on to correction, and then end with praise.

The same method will work wonders with coaching. Work with your teammate on something they are already good at with the expressed purpose of reaching an even higher level. Then, alternate to exercises so they can grow in an area where they need improvement (a weakness). Finally, after some time, move back to a different area of strength where your teammate can become even stronger.

Working with your team in this way will allow them to grow both in areas of strengths and weaknesses. It will also enable better coaching as you will not become exasperated with potentially tedious lessons.

Coaching for improvement is a task that needs to remain top of mind. Your endurance and ability here will have a long-reaching positive effect on those you are working with.

Learn From Your Trainees

Your coaching career has likely been a 360-degree learning experience. You learn from those you have coached, just as they do from you. Only foolish people believe they have nothing to learn from everyone around them. It has been my experience that a person who acts this way is often overcome with anxiety and lacks self-worth.

You need to find the actions and practices that free you of anxiety. Determine what your focus should be, specifically, what produces peace and soundness of mind within. I realize this means repeatedly considering your particular circumstances and current challenges. However, your actions and practices must be a fit for your circumstances in order to be most beneficial for your heart and mind.

It is most likely that such actions and practices will keep your emotions in check and point to a positive, though unfamiliar, direction.

"Be anxious for nothing, but in everything, by prayer and supplication with gratitude, make your requests known to God. And the peace of God, which surpasses

all understanding, will protect your hearts and minds through Christ Jesus.
Philippians 4:6-7

Do not conform to the world; instead, discern the challenges and questions before you so you can address them honestly.

Think back to what you consider the good old days. Were you accomplishing your dreams, goals, and plans? Most reading this are probably shaking their heads no. Do not let fond memories cloud your current judgment. Instead, hold fast to your dreams and remind yourself daily why you are performing the steps you put in place. Action without a consistent reminder of the target can become tiresome.

Remember Your End Goal

Reminding yourself of the end goal is one of the ways to change anxiety into joy. It is about *why* you are doing what you are doing. Remind yourself why you are doing different actions than almost everyone you know and why your circle of influence is so vital.

Your circle of influence will have a profound effect on your emotions. You need to find a circle of influence that will accompany you in fearlessness. Those characterized by fear, even on an inconsistent basis, will enable other negative emotions also.

Do not settle for less than your already established dreams and goals. When I say not to settle for less, I am talking about all areas of life: professionally, personally, relationally, and spiritually.

"But you are a chosen race, a royal priesthood, a holy nation, a people for God's own possession, so that you may declare the goodness of Him who has called you out of darkness
into His marvelous light."
1 Peter 2:9

Overcoming your emotions will influence all aspects of your life, day, night, and everything in between.

Stop now and decide to walk away from the emotional roller coaster that your friends and colleagues keep buying tickets to ride. Instead, get off the ride today and act on your desire to achieve.

The Right Time To Lead

You may be able to lead others, but can you lead them to their success? Think about that for a minute. You know that you have the ability to lead. You also know that people will follow the banner you are waving. However, is this the right time to be in a leadership position?

I am not at all talking about walking away from leadership and coaching. What I am asking you to consider is: are you the right person to be leading the group you are in charge of?

You may be authorized to lead them, but are you equipped to coach them to accomplish the shared goals of the team? Additionally, if you are qualified to coach them, is the team ready to digest and process the training?

The easy answer is a mighty YES! However, if you take a moment to consider all the moving pieces, then you may say, "I don't know," or even "Maybe." Regardless, have the self-knowledge to understand that you are not always the right person for every situation—that is maturity.

The leader who drinks platitudes is also the person who will become ill from too much of a good thing.

"Know this: in the last days perilous times will come.
Men will be lovers of themselves, lovers of money, boastful, proud, blasphemers,
disobedient to parents, unthankful, unholy, without natural affection, trucebreakers,
slanderous, unrestrained, fierce, despisers of those who are good, traitors, reckless,
conceited, lovers of pleasure more than lovers of God,
having a form of godliness, but denying its power.
Turn away from such people."
2 Timothy 3:1-5.

Seeking to reinforce your historical glory on the backs of your team will never work out well for anyone. You may have the correct answers, but if no one is asking, then why are you even responding?

Instead of forcing your leadership on others, you need to step back and carefully consider your situation. Rather than forging and pushing ahead, take time to be a model of good work for its own sake. This approach will help not only others but also yourself. Even after some success, do not think that you no longer have room for further growth.

Living as a model of good works means you will portray consistency and moderation to your team, which will teach them many lessons about integrity, dignity, and self-control. The term "killing them with kindness" is very appropriate when stepping back from the front lines of leadership and taking a more moderate approach.

Think about the lessons you want to teach your team. Are you truly living them? It is too easy to delude yourself with an attitude of "do as I say, but not as I do." You may have lived that type of life up until now, but today can be the first day you change. No one can erase your past successes. However, a true change will push you forcibly ahead toward those achievements that have been out of your reach.

Make that change, live a life of moderation, and success will come to you naturally and in due time.

Summary of Chapter 28

1. If you are going to hold people accountable, you must have an improvement process in place to be a catalyst for change.
2. Coaching people to improve their strengths brings about positive interaction and opportunities for significant growth.
3. Keeping your emotions in check allows you to discern the challenges before you and walk through them peacefully.
4. Never settle for less than you know your dreams, goals, and plans have for you in all areas of life: professional, personal, relational, and spiritual.
5. When you walk in the responsibility of the authority you have been granted, you are less likely to become a lover of self.
6. Live the moderation, and success will be drawn to you.

He who trusts in his own heart is a fool,
but whoever walks wisely will be delivered.
Proverbs 28:26

Proverbs for Leadership

Chapter 29:
You will Always Need Additional Coaching

*He who is often reproved, yet hardens his neck,
will suddenly be destroyed, and that without remedy.
Proverbs 29:1*

Regardless of how much you have achieved, you need more coaching.

Dealing With The Unexpected

Looking back on this particular coaching session that I experienced, I can now laugh at how naive I was to think that there would not be any constructive criticism. Let me explain.

Our company had monthly P&L (profit and loss) reviews. This was in the time before video conferencing. I would sit in my office and wait for the phone to ring, and, on the other end, there would be executives at our corporate office. Every other month, we flew to corporate to conduct these reviews in person. Otherwise, they were done over the phone.

I walked into this conference call feeling confident. I had crushed my numbers. Additionally, I had overachieved my forecasting from the previous month. I was ahead of my number, year to date. On top of all that, my P&L was the best it had ever been for my geographic region—period.

When the time came to go through the reports, I explained my success in great detail. Then the questions began.

Our company president was focusing on three items. We had incurred overtime costs, one medium-sized account lost money that month, and my forecast from the previous month was inaccurate. I was floored. Here was the best P&L that my geographic region had ever recorded (among the other items I already listed), and our president was nitpicking at the few issues that he could find. For the next 30 minutes, we dug deep into the overtime issue, the money-losing account, and the forecasting problem.

By the time we were done, I was frustrated and angry. The president pointed out that if I had a firmer grasp on forecasting, it would have solved the overtime and money-losing account issues. In the end, I (grudgingly) agreed verbally but not in thought.

There will be times in your life and career when what you expect does not occur. However, what does happen instead turns out better than anything you could have imagined: a seemingly negative situation turns into a positive lesson.

"This Book of the Law shall not depart from your mouth, but you shall meditate on it day and night, so that you may be careful to do according to all that is written in it. For then you will make your way prosperous, and then you will have good success."
Joshua 1:8

When The Coach Becomes The Student

Sometimes, the coach becomes the student. The long amount of time you have spent in training others is said to be a requirement, but what if you can be on the receiving end of the reward? What if the more you coach, the greater encouragement you receive? If you knew this to be accurate, how would it affect the time you spend in preparing to coach and in coaching itself?

Often, people tend to coach off the cuff. How much time do you spend each week preparing to coach your team? When I lead groups, I have a weekly team conference call with my direct reports. This is a common practice of many leaders. Some leaders like the conversation at the start of the week, while others prefer the end of it. I am an end-of-the-week kind of guy. I like to discuss how it went and how it will shape what is to come.

I would spend the days before the meeting selecting particular topics of conversation to lead my team to further excellence and also to encourage them. It is not difficult to choose subjects of discussion. Just read your email each day. I save the emails that have learning moments and opportunities into a file, and that becomes the basis of the conversation for the week.

Some of the topics are items that each of my group knows about already, while others are things that one of them experienced but that I believe would be beneficial for the group to discuss. None of the topics addressed are presented in a way to single out or shame any individual. Indeed, the opposite is true. The items are selected for the group to learn from the individual experiences over the past week. By sharing these various topics and talking through them, you may find a similar situation that you experienced and can thus respond thoughtfully in the future.

Leveraging the situations that everyone experiences every week also emphasizes that there is nothing really new. There are only new ways to process and respond to recurring issues. The challenge you experienced yesterday is likely the same one a colleague is experiencing today or will tomorrow. Why would you hide behind your (potential) embarrassment in how you reacted when you can turn it into a learning experience to teach others how to respond instead of merely reacting?

If you genuinely want to coach your team, then you will have to work on a platform of shared experiences that ultimately are about preparing for the unexpected.

Passing The Mantle

This process of coaching is far more profound than merely providing information for growth. It has the potential to pass the mantle from one individual or group to another. Back in biblical times, there were teachers and disciples, but there was also a much deeper form of discipleship. It was called the "passing of a mantle."

> *"And as they were crossing, Elijah said to Elisha, "Ask for something, and I will do it for you before I am taken away from you." And Elisha said, "Let a double portion of your spirit be upon me."*
> *2 Kings 2:9*

Some have described the actual mantle as a blanket or coat. When one passed a mantle, the teacher (coach) would pour into the student all of their learning so that this expertise becomes the starting point of knowledge and wisdom for the pupil.

Your teachings should always be profitable for general education, correction, and training.

> *"All Scripture is inspired by God and is profitable for teaching, for reproof, for correction, and for instruction in righteousness, that the man of God may be complete, thoroughly equipped for every good work."*
> *2 Timothy 3:16-17*

However, these lessons should also teach your teammates to surpass your achievements. Your role in coaching should focus on equipping your team to prepare for providing good work and solutions in every situation they may find themselves in. Teachers that do not want their students to exceed them are being short-sighted and, in my opinion, have disqualified themselves from leadership.

The moment you start worrying that your team (as a group or individually) is exceeding your abilities is when you have stopped being the leader and instead have become a blockade to progress. Doing this will turn your vision inward. Indeed, your work will become increasingly complicated since you are only looking at how to exploit it for your own good, as opposed to creating growth in your team. The lessons you have learned will become stunted in their presentation and will be repetitious in their foundational items rather than growth topics. Why is this? Because you will not challenge your team to grow and will view them as a threat that must review the same material repeatedly.

Thoughts On Self-Sabotage

Presenting your team with the same lessons time and again does not reaffirm foundational practices; rather, it stunts growth. Do you ask your team what they think of a situation or how they have considered working through it? Do you secretly hope that they do not find the answer and must rely on you?

If this is where you are, then you must seek out a neutral party and explain to them what ailment has wrapped around you like a python that squeezes the life out of its victim. To withhold information from your team is self-sabotage.

The good news is that you can cure yourself of this affliction. You do not even need to wait for any specific situation to do so. Do it now, and you will again become an inspiration to others while reaping the rewards (both apparent and unapparent).

What happens when you have a genuine heart for coaching for the benefit of others? You become something far more significant than you could have ever been on your own, regardless of how hard you work.

Generosity Of Spirit

The generous and positive person you will become will look forward to what is yet to come instead of looking back regretfully. The difference will also affect your attitude.

Instead of being morose and always looking at the worst-case scenario, you will look at most situations with joy and peace, knowing that you have worked diligently to nurture others throughout your career and life.

"Now may the Lord of peace Himself give you peace always in every way. The Lord be with you all."
2 Thessalonians 3:16

Moving forward in this way, you will experience peace through any tribulation that occurs in your life. Notice I do not say that you will not experience distress. Everyone goes through grief at some point. Nevertheless, you will face it with dignity and a mature understanding. Now, before you think I am assuming you will be some starry-eyed babbling fool, let me explain what I mean. The peace you will know when overcoming life's ordeals will be deeper when measured against similar situations in a corporate coaching context.

Yes, it is relative, but what is not? The joy you experience in any circumstance is comparable to that of others in the same situation. A positive outlook, whether in everyday life or in coaching others, will overcome any difficult situations thrown at you by the world.

This positive attitude includes fearlessness and gratitude. It means having peace about you that surpasses the understanding of others. It means not allowing yourself to be injured emotionally while at the same time being emotionally available and not living behind a wall.

Are you there already? Do you want to improve? What do you think you need to do to make a difference in your life? I will give you a hint. It is not about you. It is about how you pour your life into others and what you expect will occur.

Living that way will bring you the desired results over and over again!

Summary of Chapter 29

1. Your confidence, when acted on as arrogance, invites criticism.
2. The unexpected disappointment has the potential to teach you a lesson far more positive than you thought possible.
3. Coaching at its best is the passing of a mantle.
4. You become an obstacle to progress and growth if you are concerned anyone you are helping will exceed your abilities.
5. Everyone experiences grief; do not live there. Move on to peace and expectation.

Where there is no vision, the people perish;
but happy is he who keeps the teaching.
Proverbs 29:18

Chapter 30:
Set a Plan

*There are three things which go well, indeed, four are comely in going
a lion which is strongest among beasts and does not turn away for any; a strutting
rooster, a male goat also,
and a king, against whom there is no rising up.
Proverbs 30:29-31*

*You and your team will not get where all of you want to be, if you do not know why
and set a plan to arrive there.*

Know Your Teammates' Dreams

Let us imagine you are now the leader. You are then assigned your first team. Do you know what to do? Better yet, do you know what your purpose is? Let me tell you: it is not about you; it is all about the individuals on your team.

You may know the dreams, goals, and plans you have in mind for yourself, but what about those of your team? Do you know the purpose each one of them means to fulfill? When you spend all the time on yourself, without looking through the eyes of others, you lose the opportunity to assist them in growing and, at the same time, are sabotaging your growth. There is a plan for each of them, and you are an essential part of their success.

Your teammates each have a plan set apart for them to achieve. They may not be aware of it, but do not think less of them. Did you always know your purpose in life?

"For I know the plans that I have for you, says the Lord, plans for peace and not for evil, to give you a future and a hope."
Jeremiah 29:11

If you answered anything other than no, then you are likely lying. Please work with your team, helping them to learn, understand, and embrace their purpose.

Work On Assisting Others

In doing so, you are assisting your teammate in discovering the excellence that awaits him or her while at the same time opening up a new door to your future. Make no mistake about this, though. I am not advocating assisting others to learn their purpose simply for you to move on to a better position. Of course, when you help others, you will reap the benefits, but this should not be your motivation.

This work is about assisting others and not about what you can gain from them. It is about helping others realize their dreams and aiding them in understanding their true artistry.

"Therefore, I say to you, take no thought about your life, what you will eat, or what you will drink, nor about your body, what you will put on. Is not life more than food and the body than clothing?"
Matthew 6:25

Still, you would not be a good leader if you did not do some things for yourself. However, there is a time for everything. Now, you must focus on helping others.

Recognize Your Flaws

Think back to your early days in whatever business or group you were once associated with. Were you always leading, or did you begin like everyone else: a member of a team? Did you achieve the level of success you have today on your own, or was it because others took an interest in assisting you?

Back then, it may not have seemed as though you were supported, but now that you are beyond those years, look back and be honest with what you see.

When I look back, I see a man striving to be the best but flawed in more ways than he was willing to admit. I also see many people who, over the years, gave him assignments that allowed him to grow in wisdom, understanding, and knowledge. I am willing to bet that many of you who are reading this book see something similar in yourself.

The beginning of success is self-confidence. It is best if you believe that you are capable of succeeding whether or not you are doing so right now. You can call these positive stance expectations a good attitude, a self-fulfilling prophecy, or anything else of the like. Ultimately, you will become what you believe about yourself. Whether you think you are a success or a failure, you are correct. You will find a way to become what you believe.

See The Potential In Others

Now the role of the leader comes into play. The leader has the privilege of assisting teammates in seeing themselves as more than they currently are. Leaders must look beyond the reality of today and instead recognize the untapped potential of their teammates. As the leader, you are responsible for bringing that vision to light in your teammates' eyes.

You begin this process by taking a genuine interest in learning about your teammates and what their dreams and goals are. Doing this may be more complicated than it sounds. Depending on the person, they may not have fleshed out such plans but may still have a dream. Some people have been so down over the years that they do not even have an idea of how to start. Your duty is to encourage them toward what they cannot see in themselves.

Leave The Past Behind

I remember many times standing in front of a group of people and speaking to them about what they could be and do with their lives. Like any group of people, some eagerly accepted what I was saying, and others dismissed me outright. Regardless of their initial response, however, my message was the same. They needed to leave the past behind and not let it dictate their actions. Instead, they needed to look to the future, discover a dream, form it into a goal, and then set a written plan in place to become the success they all desired to be.

I explained to them that they would need assistance and they should not expect to do this on their own. Each would require multiple people in their corner to help them along the way. Help would not only come from other colleagues but would also come from a close-knit circle of influence to encourage and keep them aligned with the road to success.

> *"Therefore, be patient, brothers, until the coming of the Lord. Notice how the farmer waits for the precious fruit of the earth and is patient with it until he receives the early and late rain."*
> James 5:7

This circle of influence that believes in your success is vital for many reasons. They will not let you forget what you have learned; they believe in you, encourage you, and have your best interests at heart. Everyone needs a circle of influence not to do the work but to assist them to thrive.

The Challenge Of Selflessness

To make this happen, you need to make yourself vulnerable. Before that happens, though, you need to become approachable and trustworthy. As a leader, it is up to you to bring out the best in others for their future. Are you ready for that challenge?

If you are willing to take on the mantle of helping others to succeed, you will be making a genuine difference in their lives, which will create improvement and have potential generational effects on their family. Living your life with this selflessness as part of your character will also affect your own family.

Imagine the progress that will occur over generations in both families when you are willing to help another person attain their dreams. Your actions will be remembered, as you will be commended for taking an interest in others.

Your interest in others is proof you have learned the lessons that are needed for teaching, judgment, correction, and training in the right way of living and doing things. This means you have not only paid attention to those lessons but have made them your own, improving and passing them on to others.

> *"All Scripture is inspired by God and is profitable for teaching,*
> *for reproof, for correction, and for instruction in righteousness,*
> *that the man of God may be complete,*
> *thoroughly equipped for every good work."*
> 2 Timothy 3:16-17

Are You Ready?

What you have accomplished is not to be taken lightly. Most people do not consider the interests and outcomes of others. All too often today, everyone is solely concerned about themselves. I have heard it called the "me and my way of life." You have broken the mold and moved beyond that into helping others and, ultimately, making a mark not just on another family but on society as a whole.

Remember, your efforts and commitment to the leadership of others will have long-lasting effects. Make those efforts that improve the situations of others. You have the necessary skills. The question now is: are you ready to use them to help others?

Summary of Chapter 30

1. Understand the plan and purpose for your life.
2. Time spent assisting others with their plans will help you reap the rewards of your plans.
3. When you have sown into others' plans with help, expect and allow the reaping to fall into your plans.
4. The interest you take in others, and their success is proof you are ready for promotion into greater prosperity.

If you have been foolish in lifting up yourself, or if you have thought evil, put your hand on your mouth.
Proverbs 30:32

About the Author: Sean Litvak

Early in life, people told Sean Litvak he talked too much. Yet, even today, individuals sometimes marvel at all Sean has to say. Through these experiences, Sean has learned how to harness his tongue and has become far more moderated than when he was younger.

Sean discovered over the years the importance of self-talk and how running his mouth could lead to the racing of his mind and land him in self-sabotage while at the same time understanding the importance of how his words affect others. Individuals today are far more responsive and thoughtful about the words said to them, and because of the shift Sean has made in his communication, people easily get to know who he is, what he believes, and how he thinks.

This change in perspective has come through years of receiving feedback from others, sometimes encouraging and at other times discouraging or even harsh. Often, Sean heard that he had too grand of expectations for himself and others. However, it was through these interactions that Sean learned his expectations were only for himself, not others, and the expectations others had for themselves were not his to improve upon unless asked to assist with a plan.

As a natural talker that can easily mix in networking and social settings, Sean had to learn the importance of listening to others and not just engaging them in conversation. When you read anything, Sean has authored or heard him speak, you have most likely heard him talk about how "God made us with two ears and one mouth for a reason. Listen more than you speak!"

His understanding of the value of listening has created an atmosphere that motivates others to group engagement and produced enjoyment on teams where Sean either leads or is an active participant following other leaders.

Sean subscribes to the philosophy that all leaders must be followers first before they earn areas of leadership authority. He also believes that even once someone achieves a leadership role, it is best for individuals to participate in other organizations or groups as team members, not the leader. Ultimately, Sean believes that always being in submission to another leader produces growth that is not found in self-improvement studies or only leading and not following.

Sean is passionate about understanding yourself and improving. He leverages the technology around him to gain greater wisdom, understanding, and knowledge about how to achieve the goals he has set for himself, helping others with the goals they want to achieve, and writing plans to create actionable steps for those goals.

Sean Litvak is a native of the Chicagoland area, a graduate of the University of Illinois – Urbana/Champaign and currently lives in southern Indiana outside Louisville, KY, with his wife, Lauren.

Connect with Sean Litvak
Website: www.litvakleadership.com
Email: sean.litvak@litvakleadership.com

Sean Litvak

Join the Proverbs For Leadership Community

Made in the USA
Columbia, SC
08 April 2023